The Gift of Prayer

The GIFT OF PRAYER

*A Treasury
of Personal Prayer
from the
World's Spiritual
Traditions*

A Fellowship in Prayer Book
CONTINUUM ✦ NEW YORK

1995
The Continuum Publishing Company
370 Lexington Avenue
New York, NY 10017

*The Gift of Prayer: A Treasury of Personal Prayer from the
World's Spiritual Traditions*
Compiled and edited by Jared T. Kieling

Printed in the United States of America

Library of Congress Cataloging-in-Publication Data

The gift of prayer : a treasury of personal prayer from the world's
    spiritual traditions.
        p.   cm.
    "A Fellowship in prayer book."
    Includes bibliographical references and indexes.
    ISBN 0-8264-0837-0 (alk. paper)
    1. Prayers. I. Fellowship in prayer.
  BL560.G54   1995
291.4'3—dc20   95–12852
                                                          CIP

Contents

CONTENTS

Contents

Introduction

———————

Mystics have gone to mountains and deserts to find the sacred space best suited to communion with God. Pilgrims have gone to cathedrals, shrines, and temples. Most of us, however, pray to our God in the kitchen, on the subway, or by the bank of a stream.

Regardless of our particular faith tradition, we have found that meditation and prayer lead us away from the ego, with its demands for power, possessions and worldly success, and into the depths of our being. There we can reconnect with the divine energy that enables us to act with loving kindness toward each other and all of God's creation.

Through that healing experience we become more joyous, more peaceful, more hopeful, and more caring and compassionate toward ourselves and each person we meet. And we become channels through which those divine qualities become manifest in the world. We once again experience our inter-relatedness with all humankind and feel the impulse to help each other in every way we can. When we pray we set into motion vast, invisible energies from which visible effects have always flowed, and always will.

What prayers should we use? That's up to us. Much of the world's most beautiful literature is sacred literature, coming down to us through the centuries from all the world's faith traditions. You will find a great many of those prayers in this book. Prayers that might express your hope, your suffering, your joy, your gratitude.

Fellowship in Prayer, the bi-monthly, interfaith journal, is another source of beautiful and moving prayers. Each issue offers prayers from a variety of authors, well known and unknown, ancient and contemporary.

Every sincere prayer is as valuable as another. There are three principles, however, that spiritual leaders in all ages have found to be of particular value to our spiritual life and the effectiveness of our prayers:

- ✦ *Pray with gratitude.* If we reflect on the blessings of our life—starting with the fact that we are alive—we realize how very much we have to be grateful for. Gratitude and giving thanks for what we have—and for what it is in us to be—are at the heart of effective prayer.

- ✦ *Look forward to praying.* The time you spend in prayer and meditation can become the most celebratory time of your day. Since we don't spend that much time praying, the time we do spend is precious. Don't let your prayer and meditation become routine or feel like a duty. Cultivate an attitude of joyfulness about this wonderful opportunity to spend time with the source of your being.

- ✦ *Have confidence in prayer.* Never underestimate the power of prayer. Prayer recalls us to our inner blessedness. It reminds us of God's love, the sure foundation of our being. It leads us to the deep reservoir of spiritual power within us that is available always for helping us, our family, our neighbors, our Mother Earth. We can't foresee the answer to our prayers, nor should we demand instant satisfaction of all our desires and complaints. What we *can* do through prayer is to open ourselves to the amazing grace that will bless and sustain us all the days of our lives.

The prayers in this book were selected for their simplicity, beauty and power of expression, and above all for their usefulness as prayers we might actually use in our time. The book is made like a string of beads, arranged so that each prayer, unique though it is, touches the ones beside it in some way, even though they may have been brought together from widely separated centuries and richly contrasting cultures. Titles applied to them are for the most part additions of the editor, as an aid to reference.

The headings under which the prayers are organized in the table of contents show only one pattern into which they can be seen to fall. There are endless other resonances to be found, and you will discover them as you read and reread these prayers. These great world devotions become, like a long rope of pearls, warmer and more lustrous with frequent touch.

To help you make your own connections, to help you find a prayer for a particular occasion or problem, and to enable you to revisit prayers whose location or title you may not recall, *The Gift of Prayer* has included a subject index.

The Gift of Prayer

*Prayer is a powerful thing, for God
has bound and tied Himself thereto.*
—*Martin Luther*

Telling God's Greatness

Adoration and Praise

✦

Awe Before the Created World

✦

As Dawn Follows the Night

✦

The Thirst for God

✦

Silence

Adoration and Praise

*I have so many things to do today that I shall
spend the first three hours in prayer.*
—Martin Luther

Exult

1   Let everything that breathes praise God!

Psalm 150:6

Let Us Wake Up the Universe

2   The whole world is asleep, and God so full of goodness, so great, so worthy of all praise, no one is thinking of Him! See, nature praises Him, and man . . . who ought to praise Him, sleeps! Let us go, let us go and wake up the universe . . . and sing His praises!

Blessed Mariam Baouardy

Thou

3   Wherever I go—only Thou! Wherever I stand—only Thou! Just Thou; again Thou; always Thou!

Hasidic Song

---

4   *Let the conch shell, the kettle drum,*
the hand drum, and the horn
sound, and keep you, O God,
awake.

Eknath

Lord of Glory

5   Glorious Lord, I give you greeting!
Let the church and the chancel praise you,
Let the plain and the hillside praise you,
Let the dark and daylight praise you,
Let the birds and the honeybees praise you,
Let the male and female praise you,
And I shall praise you, Lord of glory:
Glorious Lord, I give you greeting!

Welsh prayer

Beginning Nor End

6   O Lord, giver and ruler of the world,
even while the earth was unformed you were King
and still will you reign when all things are
brought to an end.
You are supreme.
You will never be equalled.
You are power and might:
there is neither beginning nor end in you.

Jewish prayer

Praise God in the Earth Our Mother

7   O praise God in his holy place,
    praise him in the sky our tent,
    praise him in the earth our mother;
    Praise him for his mighty works,
    praise him for his marvelous power.
    Praise him with the beating of great drums,
    praise him with the horn and rattle;
    Praise him in the rhythm of the dance,
    praise him in the clapping of the hands;
    Praise him in the stamping of the feet,
    praise him in the singing of the chant.
    Praise him with the rushing of great rivers,
    praise him with the music of the wind;
    Praise him with the swaying of tall trees,
    praise him with the singing of the sea.
    Praise him, the one on whom we lean and do not
       fall;
  Let everything that has breath praise the Lord.

A Psalm for Africa (Psalm 150:6)

Pray

8   More things are wrought by prayer
    Than this world dreams of.
    Wherefore, let thy voice
    Rise like a fountain for me night and day.

Alfred, Lord Tennyson

Kmvoum

9   In the beginning was Kmvoum
Today is Kmvoum,
Tomorrow will be Kmvoum.
Who can make an image of Kmvoum?
He has no body.
He is as a word which comes out of your mouth.
That word! It is no more.
It is past and still it lives!
So is Kmvoum.

Pygmy praise-poem from Zaire

Always You

10   Where I wander—you!
Where I ponder—you!
Only you, you again, always you!
You! You! You!
When I am gladdened—you!
When I am saddened—you!
Only you, you again, always you!
You! You! You!
Sky is you, earth is you!
You above! You below!
In every trend, at every end,
Only you, you again, always you!
You! You! You!

Levi Yitzchak of Berditchev

O My Soul

11 Bless the Lord, O my soul, and all that is within me, praise his holy name.

Psalm 103:1

From Within

12 How sublime—   *Arigata ya*
a boat beneath the moon   *tsuki no funauta*
and from within, a prayer. *Namu Amida*

Kozan, eighteenth-century
Japanese poet

---

13 *My God and my all.*

Saint Francis of Assisi

This World at Thy Feet

14   In one salutation to Thee, my God, let all my
senses spread out and touch this world at Thy feet.
Like a rain-cloud of July hung low with its burden
of unshed showers let all my mind bend down at
Thy door in one salutation to Thee.
Let all my songs gather together their diverse
strains into a single current and flow to a sea of
silence in one salutation to Thee.
Like a flock of homesick cranes flying night and
day back to their mountain nests let all my life
take its voyage to its eternal home in one
salutation to Thee.

Rabindranath Tagore

That Which Is Below

15   Great Spirit, piler up of rocks into towering
       mountains!
When you stamp on the stone,
   the dust rises and fills the land.
Hardness of the precipice;
Waters of the pool that run into misty rain when
       stirred.
Vessel overflowing with oil!
Father who sews the heavens like cloth:
Let him knit together that which is below.

Shona prayer, Zimbabwe

Bahá'í Prayer

16 Blessed is the spot, and the house, and the place, and the city, and the heart, and the mountain, and the refuge, and the cave, and the valley, and the land, and the sea, and the island, and the meadow where mention of God has been made, and His praise glorified.

Bahá'u'lláh

All Things

17 How great are God's riches! How deep are his wisdom and knowledge! Who can explain his decisions? Who can understand his ways . . . for all things were created by him, and all things exist through him and for him. To God be the glory for ever! Amen.

From Saint Paul's
Letter to the Romans

The God of Heaven

18 The might of all rivers in the world is not to be
        compared with that of the sea;
The dignity of rivers which rise on the hill is not
        as that of the lagoon.
There is no Ifa that can be compared with Eji-
        Ogbe;
To command is the privilege of a commander;
Eji-Ogbe, you are the king of them all.
I asked for honors from the lagoon, for he is
        greater than the river.
I received them, but I was not satisfied.
I asked them at the hands of Olokun Jeniade, the
        God of the sea and father of all rivers,
But still I was not satisfied.
Who does not know that only the gifts of
        Olorun,
        the God of Heaven,
Are sufficient till the day of one's death?

Prayer of the Yoruba
people of Nigeria

The Shema

19 Hear, O Israel,
The Lord our God, the Lord is one.
Blessed is his name,
whose glorious kingdom is forever.

The Torah

Blessed

20   My God, the soul You have given me is pure,
for You created it,
You formed it and You made it life within me.
You watch over it within me,
but one day you will take it from me to
everlasting life.
My God and God of my fathers,
as long as the soul is within me, I will declare
that You are the master of all deeds,
the ruler of all creatures and
the Lord of every soul.
Blessed are You, Lord,
who brings the dead into everlasting life.

Jewish morning prayer

Let Heaven Praise the Lord

21   Praise the Lord from the heavens:
praise him, in the heights,
praise him, all his angels,
praise him, all his armies!

Praise him, sun and moon,
praise him, all you stars of light
praise him, heavens above heavens,
and waters above the heavens!

Let them praise the name of the Lord:
for he commanded, and they were created;
he has established them in their places for ever
by a decree that shall never pass away.

Let praise go forth from the earth,
dragons, and all the deeps:
fire and hailstones, snow and mist,
storms that do his will,

mountains and hills,
fruit trees and all cedars,
wild animals and the cattle of man,
creeping things and flying birds,

all kings on earth, and all nations,
princes—all rulers of the world,
young men and maidens,
all elders and children!

Let them all praise the name of the Lord:
for his name and no other is exalted,
his splendor is above all earth and heaven.
He has raised up the fortunes of his people
    the praises of all his saints of Israel,
    the people dear unto his heart.

Praise the Lord!

Psalm 148

Wonders

22 Who is like you, revealing the deeps,
    Fearful in praises, doing wonders?

    The creator who discovers all from nothing
    Is revealed to the heart, but not to the eye;
    Therefore ask not who nor where—
    For God fills heaven and earth.

                    Judah Halevi

The Compassionate, the Merciful

23 Praise be to Allah, the Lord of the worlds!
    The Compassionate, the Merciful!
    King on the day of reckoning!
    You only do we worship, and you only
        do we ask for help.
    Guide us along the straight path,
    The path of those to whom you have been
    gracious;
        with whom you are not angry
        and who go not astray.

                    Daily prayer, from the first sūra
                    of the Qur'an

Whoso'er Thou Art

24   O thou that stayst the earth and hast thy firm
     throne thereon: whoso'er thou art, unfathomable
     to human knowledge
     whether thou art Zeus
     or the necessity of Nature
     or the mind of man—
     to thee I raise my voice.

                    Euripides

High Heaven

25   How does the Moon wax?
     How does the Moon wane?
     Fifteen days does the Moon wax.
     Fifteen days does the Moon wane.
     So long is the waning, even as the waxing. . . .
     Who is it, through whom the Moon
        waxes and wanes, other than You?

                    Zoroastrian litany to the Moon

The Mystery

26   I am the wind which breathes upon the sea,
I am the wave of the ocean
I am the murmur of the billows,
I am the ox of the seven combats,
I am the vulture upon the rocks,
I am a beam of the sun,
I am the fairest of plants,
I am the wild boar in valor,
I am a salmon in the water,
I am a lake in the plain,
I am a word of science,
I am the point of the lance of battle,
I am the God who created in the head the fire of
      thought.
Who is it who throws light into the meeting on
      the mountain?
Who announces the ages of the moon?
Who teaches the place where couches the sun?
            (If not I)

            Pre-Christian Irish prayer
            ascribed to Amergin,
            The Book of Invasions

Awe Before the Created World

O God who made this beautiful earth,
when will it be ready to receive your saints?
How long, O Lord, how long?
—George Bernard Shaw

Hymn to Amon Ra

27 Hail to thee, Amon Ra, Lord of the thrones of
the earth; the oldest existence, ancient of heaven,
support of all things;
Chief of the gods, Lord of truth; father of the
gods, maker of men and beasts and herbs; maker
of all things above and below;
Deliverer of the sufferer and oppressed, judging
the poor;
Lord of wisdom, Lord of mercy; most loving,
opener of every eye, source of joy, in whose
goodness the gods rejoice, thou whose name is
hidden.
Thou art the one, maker of all that is, the one;
the only one; maker of gods and men; giving
food to all.

Hail to thee, thou one with many heads; sleepless
where all others sleep, adoration to thee.
Hail to thee from all creatures from every land,
from the height of heaven, from the depths of
the sea.
The spirits thou hast made extol thee, saying,
welcome to thee, father of the fathers of the gods;
we worship thy spirit which is in us.

> Ancient Egyptian psalm to the
> Lord of Lords

Lord Everlasting

28 Praise we the Lord
Of the heavenly kingdom,
God's power and wisdom,
The works of His hand;
As the Father of glory,
Eternal Lord,
Wrought the beginning
Of all His wonders!
Holy Creator!
Warder of men!
First, for a roof,
O'er the children of earth,
He established the heavens,
And founded the world,
And spread the dry land
For the living to dwell in.
Lord Everlasting!
Almighty God!

> Caedmon

Every Creature a Hymn

29   O you who covers the high places with waters,
  who sets the sand as a bound to the sea and
upholds all things:
  the sun sings your praises, the moon gives
you glory,
  Every creature offers a hymn to you, his
author and creator forever.

Eastern Orthodox prayer

The Canticle of the Sun

30   O Most High, Almighty, good Lord God, to you
belong praise, glory, honor, and all blessing!

Praised be my Lord God for all his creatures, and
especially for our brother the sun, who brings us
the day and who brings us the light; fair is he and
shines with a very great splendor: O Lord, to us
he signifies you!

Praised be my Lord for our sister the moon, and
for the stars, which He has set clear and lovely in
heaven.

Praised be my Lord for our brother the wind, and
for the air and cloud, calms and all weather by
which you uphold life in all creatures.

Praised be my Lord for our sister water, who is very serviceable to us and humble and precious and clean.

Praised be my Lord for our brother fire, through whom you give us light in the darkness; and he is bright and pleasant and very mighty and strong.

Praised be my Lord for our mother the earth, who sustains and keeps us, and brings forth fruits and flowers of many colors, and grass.

Praised be my Lord for all those who pardon one another for His love's sake, and who endure weakness and tribulation; blessed are they who peaceably endure, for you, O most High, shall give them a crown.

Praised be my Lord for our sister, the death of the body, from which no one escapes.

Woe to him who dies in mortal sin!

Blessed are they who are found walking by your most holy will, for the second death shall have no power to do them harm.

Praise you and bless the Lord, and give thanks unto God, and serve God with great humility.

Saint Francis of Assisi

Litany to the Greatness of the Waters

31 All the shores around the Sea Vourukasha are in
          commotion.
    The whole middle is bubbling up
    When she flows forth unto them,
    When she streams forth unto them,
    Aredvi Sura Anahita.
    To whom belong a thousand lakes,
    To whom a thousand deltas:
    Any one of these lakes,
    Any one of these outlets,
    Is a forty days' ride
    For a man mounted on a good horse.

Zoroastrian manuscript

Holy Groves

32 How lovely are thy holy groves
          God of heaven and earth
    My soul longs and faints
          for the circle of thy trees.
    My heart and my flesh
          sing with joy to thee
              O God of life.

Chinook Psalter

Thank You Father

33 Thank you Father for your free gift of fire.
Because it is through fire that you draw near to us
    every day.
It is with fire that you constantly bless us.
Our Father, bless this fire today.
With your power enter into it.
Make this fire a worthy thing.
A thing that carries your blessing.
Let it become a reminder of your love.
A reminder of life without end.
Make the life of these people to be baptized like
    this fire.
A thing that shines for the sake of people.
A thing that shines for your sake.
Father, heed this sweet-smelling smoke.
Make their life also sweet smelling.
A thing sweet smelling that rises to God.
A holy thing.
A thing fitting for you.

Masai prayer, Tanzania

Blessing Unto the Fire

34 O Fire! Son of the most high!
Worthy of sacrifice, worthy of prayer!
In the dwellings of men,
Happiness may there be unto that one
Who shall sacrifice unto you
    with fuel in his hand.

Zoroastrian litany

At First

35 There was at first no Being. . . .

There was no air, nor sky beyond. . . .
There was no death, nor deathless state,
no night, no day.
The One breathed, without breath
by its own power.
There was nothing else: no, nothing else.

Darkness lay wrapped in darkness.
All was water, all over.
Love began, at first; desire
was the seed of mind.

Sages and poets, searching within,
saw the link of Being in non-Being.
But who really knows? Who can tell—
How it was born, where creation began?
The gods came later: Who then knows
That from which creation came,
Whether founded well or not?

He who sees from heaven above,
He only knows. Or, He too knows it not!

Hindu song of creation

Praise Hymn

36 Praise God, from whom all blessings flow,
    Praise Him, all creatures here below;
    Praise Him above, ye heavenly host,
    Praise Father, Son and Holy Ghost.

Thomas Ken, Bishop
of Bath and Wells

Pied Beauty

37 Glory be to God for dappled things—
    For skies of couple-colour as a brinded cow
    For rose-moles all in stipple upon trout that swim;
    Fresh-firecoal chestnut-falls, finches' wings;
    Landscape plotted and pieced—fold, fallow and
    plough;
    And all trades, their gear and tackle and trim.
    All things counter, original, spare, strange;
    Whatever is fickle, freckled (who knows how?)
    With swift, slow; sweet, sour; adazzle, dim;
    He fathers-forth whose beauty is past change:
                                        Praise Him

Gerard Manley Hopkins

All Things Bright and Beautiful

38 All things bright and beautiful,
    All creatures, great and small,
    All things wise and wonderful,
    The Lord God made them all.

Cecil Frances Alexander

You Have Given Me All

39 O God, you have formed heaven and earth;
    You have given me all the goods that the earth
         bears!
    Here is your part, my God.
    Take it!

Pygmy prayer, Zaire

All Things

40 Let the beauty of the land deepen my joy
    as well as my sorrow,
    and thus draw me closer to you,
    my Lord and my Redeemer.

Henri Nouwen

The First Blessing

41 Blessed are You, O Lord our God,
King of the universe
who feeds the whole world with
Your goodness, grace, kindness and mercy.
You give food to all flesh,
for Your mercy endures forever.
Through Your great goodness,
we have never lacked food:
may it never fail us,
for the sake of Your great Name,
for You nourish and sustain all beings,
and do good to all,
and provide food for all Your creatures
whom You have created.
Blessed are You, O Lord,
who gives food to all.

Jewish grace after meals

Thanks

42 The eyes of all wait upon Thee O Lord,
and Thou givest them their food in due season.
Thou openest Thy hand and fillest all things
living with plenteousness.

Ancient Armenian Liturgy

That Is the Story of Your Grace

43 Lord,
    I sing your praise,
    The whole day through until the night.
    Father's nets are filled,
    I have helped him.
    We have drawn them in,
    Stamping the rhythm with our feet,
    the muscles tense.
    We have sung your praise.
    On the beach, there were our mothers,
    Who bought the blessing out of the nets,
    Out of the nets into their basins.
    They rushed to the market,
    Returned and bought again.
    Lord, what a blessing is the sea
    With fish in plenty.
    Lord, that is the story of your grace.
    Nets tear, and we succumb
    Because we cannot hold them.
    Lord, with your praise we drop off to sleep.
    Carry us through the night,
    Make us fresh for the morning.
    Hallelujah for the day!
    And blessing for the night!
    Amen.

                    Ghanaian fisherman's prayer

The Generative God

44   Cattle browse peacefully
     Trees and plants are verdant,
     Birds fly from their nests
     And lift up their wings in your praise.
     All animals frisk upon their feet
     All winged things fly and alight once more—
     They come to life with your rising.

     Boats sail upstream and boats sail downstream,
     At your coming every highway is opened.
     Before your face the fish leap up from the river,
     Your rays reach the green ocean.
     You it is who place the male seed in woman,
     Who create the semen in man;
     You quicken the sun in his mother's belly
     Soothing him so that he shall not cry.
     Even in the womb you are his nurse.
     You give breath to all your creation,
     Opening the mouth of the newborn
     and giving him nourishment.

                    From the Pharaoh Akhenaton's
                    "Hymn to the Sun"

May My Prayer Be Beautiful

45   The garden is rich with diversity
With plants of a hundred families
In the space between the trees
With all the colors and fragrances.
Basil, mint and lavender,
God keep my remembrance pure,
Raspberry, Apple, Rose,
God fill my heart with love,
Dill, anise, tansy,
Holy winds blow in me.
Rhododendron, zinnia,
May my prayer be beautiful
May my remembrance O God be as incense
     to thee
In the sacred grove of eternity
As I smell and remember
The ancient forests of earth.

Chinook Psalter

Nature

46   As thou hast set the moon in the sky
to be the poor man's lantern,
so let thy Light shine in my dark life
and lighten my path;

as the rice is sown in the water
and brings forth grain in great abundance,
so let thy word be sown in our midst
that the harvest may be great;

and as the banyan sends forth its branches
to take root in the soil
so let thy Life take root in our lives.

Author unknown

Creation

47   The beauty of the trees,
     the softness of the air,
     the fragrance of the grass,
          speaks to me.

     The summit of the mountain,
     the thunder of the sky,
     the rhythm of the sea,
          speaks to me.

     The faintness of the stars,
     the freshness of the morning,
     the dewdrop in the flower,
          speaks to me.

     The strength of the fire,
     the taste of the salmon,
     the trail of the sun,
     and the life that never goes away,
          they speak to me.

     And my heart soars.

Chief Dan George

Beyond

48 Eternal, Incomprehensible God, I believe, and
    confess, and adore Thee, as being infinitely more
    wonderful, resourceful, and immense, than this
    universe which I see.

John Henry Newman

Sacred

49 I'm an Indian
    I think about common things like this pot.
    The bubbling water comes from the rain cloud.
    It represents the sky.
    The fire comes from the sun
    which warms us all, men, animals, trees.
    The meat stands for the four-legged creatures,
    our animal brothers,
    who gave of themselves so that we should live.
    The steam is living breath.
    It was water, now it goes up to the sky,
    becomes a cloud again.
    These things are sacred.
    Looking at that pot full of good soup,
    I am thinking how, in this simple manner,
    The Great Spirit takes care of me.

John Lame Deer

America

50   O beautiful for spacious skies,
      for amber waves of grain;
      for purple mountains' majesty,
      above the fruited plain.
      America, America,
      God shed his grace on thee,
      and crown thy good with brotherhood
      from sea to shining sea.

Katherine Lee Bates

Part of It

51   The mountains, I become part of it . . .
      The herbs, the fir tree,
      I become part of it.
      The morning mists,
      The clouds, the gathering waters,
      I become part of it.
      The wilderness, the dew drops, the pollen . . .
      I become part of it.

Navajo chant

Rapids

52   Most great and glorious God, who appointed the
rivers to hasten to the sea:

Make the stream of our will perpetually to flow a
cheerful and impetuous course;

bearing down all impediments of affliction,
pleasure, or self-interest;

till it plunge in the unfathomable ocean of your
love.

Charles Howe

Wildness

53   What would the world be, once bereft
Of wet and of wildness? Let them be left,
O let them be left, wildness and wet;
Long live the weeds and the wilderness yet.

Gerard Manley Hopkins

I Am

54   I am the one whose praise echoes on high.
     I adorn all the earth.
     I am the breeze that nurtures all things green.
     I encourage blossoms to flourish with ripening
         fruits.
     I am led by the spirit to feed the purest streams.
     I am the rain coming from the dew
        that causes the grasses to laugh with
        the joy of life.
     I am the yearning for good.

Saint Hildegard of Bingen

---

55   *Sitting at the edge of the lake, I*
     thought to myself, "This great
     loving gift has come to me. Let me
     lovingly drink it."

Eknath

This Earth, Our Home

56 O God, we thank you for this earth, our home;
    for the wide sky and the blessed sun,
    for the salt sea and the running water,
    for the everlasting hills and the never-resting
        winds,
    for trees and the common grass underfoot.

We thank you for our sense by which we hear the
        songs of birds,
and see the splendor of the summer fields,
and taste of the autumn fruits
and rejoice in the feel of the snow,
and smell the breath of the spring.

Grant us a heart wide open to all this beauty;
and save our souls from being so blind
that we pass unseeing when even the common
        thornbush
is aflame with your glory.

O God our creator,
who lives and reigns
for ever and ever.

Walter Rauschenbusch

As Dawn Follows the Night

*There is a light that shines beyond all things on
earth, beyond us all, beyond the heavens, beyond the
highest, the very highest heavens. This is the light
that shines in our hearts.*
—*Chandogya Upanishad*

*There is great joy in darkness.
Deepen it.*
—*Sanai*

*O lead my spirit, O raise it
from these weary depths.*
—*Ludwig van Beethoven*

Brightness

57   The Lord shall light my candle and make my
darkness to be light.

Psalm 18

Let Me Pass the Day in Peace

58   O God, you have let me pass the night in peace,
Let me pass the day in peace.
Wherever I may go
Upon my way which you made peaceable for me,
O God, lead my steps.
When I have spoken,
Keep falsehood away from me.
When I am hungry,
Keep me from murmuring.
When I am satisfied,
Keep me from pride.
Calling upon you, I pass the day,
O Lord who has no Lord.

Boran people of Kenya

Awakening

59   Great mystery of sleep,
Which has safely brought us to the beginning of
        this day
We thank you for the refreshment you daily
        provide,
And for the renewing cycle of your dreams
Which shelter our fantasies, nourish our vision,
        and purge our angers and fears.
We bless you for providing a new beginning
Whose perennial grace is tangible hope
        for all the children of earth.

We praise the gift of another morning,
And pray that we may be worthy bearers of its
    trust
    in the hours to come.
May life protect us and surprise us
And be no more harsh than our spirits may bear
Until we rest again in the vast emptiness
    of your everlasting arms.

Congregation of Abraxas

This Day

60 Grant us, O Lord, to pass this day in gladness
    and in peace
    without stumbling and without stain;
That, reaching the eventide
    victorious over all temptation,
We may praise you, the eternal God,
Who is blessed, and who governs all things,
World without end.

Mozarabic Liturgy

Morning Hymn

61   O our mother the earth, O our father the sky,
     Your children are we, and with tired backs
     We bring you gifts that you love.
     Then weave for us a garment of brightness;
     May the warp be the white light of morning,
     May the weft be the red light of evening,
     May the fringes be the falling rain,
     May the border be the standing rainbow.
     Weave for us this garment of brightness
     That we may walk fittingly where grass is green,
     O our mother the earth, O our father the sky!

               Tewa Pueblo prayer

Light

62   O God, who divides the day from the night,
     Separate our deeds from the gloom of darkness,
     That ever meditating on things holy,
     We may continually live in your light.

               Leonine Sacramentary

Evening

63 In faith let us beseech the Lord
That we may pass in peace the evening
that is drawing nigh
And the night that is to come.

Ancient Armenian Liturgy

Twilight

64 Blessed are You, Lord our God, king of the
universe.

By His word He brings on the evening twilight;
in wisdom he opens the gates of dawn,
and with foresight makes times pass and
seasons change, according to His plan.
He creates day and night,
turning light into darkness and darkness into
light.
He makes the day fade away and brings on the
night,
and separates day and night,
for He is the Lord of the hosts of heaven.

Blessed are You, Lord, who brings on the evening
twilight.

Jewish prayer for the evening

Surely, as Night Follows Dawn

65   O God, Who by making the evening to succeed
the day
>> has bestowed the gift of repose on human
>> weakness;
Grant, we beseech You, that while we enjoy these
timely blessings,
We may acknowledge the One from Whom they
come.

Mozarabic Liturgy

For Sleeping

66   God, save us.
God, hide us.
When we sleep, God do not sleep.
If we sleep, God do not get drowsy.
Tie us around your arm, God,
like a bracelet.

Samburu people of Kenya

67   *The Lord almighty grant us a quiet*
      night and a perfect end.

                    From the Office for Compline

Evening Prayer

68   Watch, dear Lord,
       with those who wake, or watch, or weep tonight,
       and give your angels charge over those who sleep.
       Tend your sick ones, O Lord Christ,
       rest your weary ones.
       Bless your dying ones.
       Soothe your suffering ones.
       Pity your afflicted ones.
       Shield your joyous ones.
       And all for your love's sake,
       Amen.

                    Saint Augustine

Day Is Done

69   Day is done.
Gone the sun

From the lake
From the hills
From the sky.

All is well,
Safely rest:

God is nigh.

Lyrics to "Taps"

Daily Prayer

70   In the evening, and morning, and noonday,
we praise you, we bless you, we thank you,
and we pray to you, Master of all,
to direct our prayer
as incense before you;
And let not our hearts turn away
to words or thoughts of wickedness,
but rescue us from all things that hunt our souls.
For to you, Lord, Lord, our eyes look up,
and our hope is in you.

Vespers of the Eastern Church

Sleep

71 Sweet Spirit of Sleep, who brings peace and rest
to weary bodies,
>   Empty us of aches and pains,
>   for we struggle as seeds through unyielding
>   earth.
Bring to us the timeless nature of your presence—
the endless void of our slumber.
>   Make us aware of the work we can do while
>   in your time
>   Make us to know our dreaming,
>   where past and future are reconciled.
Come let us honor sleep, that knits up
the raveled sleeve of care, the death of each day's
life,
sore labor's bath, balm of hurt minds,
great nature's second course,
chief nourisher in life's feast.

Congregation of Abraxas

Wake

72 Keep us, Lord, so awake in the duties of our
callings that we may thus sleep in your peace and
wake in your glory.

John Donne

Let Me Pass the Night in Peace

73 O God, you have let me pass the day in peace,
Let me pass the night in peace,
O Lord who has no Lord.
There is no strength but in you.
You alone have no obligation.
Under your hand I pass the night.
You are my father and my mother.
Amen.

Boran people of Kenya

Behold!

74 Behold! In the creation of the heavens and the
earth
and in the alternation of the night and day
are signs of understanding for humankind.

The Qur'an, sūra 190

The Thirst for God

*If you meditate on your ideal, you will acquire its
nature. If you think of God day and night, you will
acquire the nature of God.*
—Sri Ramakrishna

The Amidah

75 Lord, open my lips
and my mouth shall declare Your praise!

> From the Jewish thrice-daily
> prayer

A Prayer of Awe

76 You, O eternal Trinity, are a deep sea into which,
    the more I enter, the more I find, and the more I
    find, the more I seek.
        O abyss,
            O eternal Godhead,
                O sea profound,
    what more could you give me than yourself?
    Amen.

                Saint Catherine of Siena

Hindu Prayer

77 Just as a soul longs to meet some loved one,
    Just as a fish feels when it lies where there is no
        water,
    So is my life when separated from you.
    Hasten to my help, O protector-of-the-needy.

                Dinkar

Late Have I Loved You

78 Late have I loved you, O beauty so ancient and so
    new. Too late have I loved you! You were within
    me while I had gone outside to seek you.
    Unlovely myself, I fell heedlessly upon all those
    lovely things you had made. And always you

were with me, and I was not with you.
And all these beauties that held me far from you
would have existed not at all
unless they had their being in you!

You called, you cried, you broke open my
deafness.
You blazed, you gleamed, you drove away my
blindness.
You sent your fragrance, and I drew in my breath,
and I pant for you.

I tasted, and now I hunger and thirst. You
touched me, and now I burn with longing for
your peace.

Saint Augustine

Beyond Coming and Going

79 I came to find you, Lord;
I lived to find you.
I leave to find you.

O Lord, I took leave to know you.
I live to know you.
I have come to know you.

O Lord, show me your true face
    and mine
  before I die.

Fom a prayer by
Lama Surya Das

Friend to Me

80　O God, Thou art more friend to me
than I am to myself.
I dedicate myself to Thee,
O Lord.

'Abdu'l-Bahá

Nativity

81　What shall I give him
　　Poor as I am?
If I were a shepherd
　　I would bring a lamb;
If I were a wise man
　　I would do my part;
Yet what can I give him—
　　Give my heart.

Christina Rossetti

A Longing to Be With You

82 Give me, good Lord, a longing to be with you,
not for the avoiding of the calamities of this
world, nor so much for the attaining of the joys
of heaven, as for very love of you.

> Thomas More, from a prayer
> written a few days before his
> execution

Sacred Love

83 O Thou who camest from above,
The pure celestial fire to impart,
Kindle a flame of sacred love
On the mean altar of my heart.

> Charles Wesley

Outpouring

84 My God, I love you.

> Saint Thérèse of Lisieux on her
> deathbed

The Soul

85   Narrow is the mansion of my soul; let it be
enlarged that you may enter. It is in ruins; do
repair it. It has within it what must offend your
eyes; I confess it and know it. But who shall
cleanse it? To whom should I cry except
to you? . . .

Saint Augustine

Take, Lord, All My Liberty

86   Take, Lord, all my liberty,
        my memory, my understanding,
            and my whole will.
You have given me all that I have,
        all that I am,
            and I surrender all to Your Divine will.
Give me only Your love and Your grace.
        With this I am rich enough,
            and I have no more to ask.
Amen.

Saint Ignatius of Loyola

To Serve

87   It is glory enough for me
That I should be Your servant
It is grace enough for me
That You should be my Lord.

Arabic prayer

A Desire for God

88   O Lord, give me eyes
Which see nothing but thy glory.
Give me a mind
That finds delight in thy service.
Give me a soul
Drunk in the wine of thy wisdom.

O Lord, to find thee is my desire,
But to comprehend thee is beyond my strength.
Remembering thee is solace to my sorrowing
    heart;
Thoughts of thee are my constant companions.
I call upon thee night and day.
The flame of thy love glows
In the darkness of my night. . . .

Ansari of Herat

Silence

When you pray, do not use many words; for your
father knows what things you need
before you ask him.
—Jesus of Nazareth (Matthew 6:7-8)

Acquire inward peace, and a multitude around you
will find their salvation.
—Saint Seraphim

Plea of the Disciples of Jesus

89   Lord, teach us to pray.

Luke 11:1

Listening

90   Speak, Lord, your servant is listening.

1 Samuel 3

Be Still

91   Be still and know that I am God.

Psalm 46:10

Centering Prayer

92   There are times when I am with You
When there is no beginning or ending of time:
When the day is dateless
And the rhythm of time
Has ceased to record the hours
And the calendar, the days;
When no birds sing, but rest;
And no winds blow, but breathe.
And the air is drenched
With the white silence of love
And my fingers trace
The lineaments of Your Face.

Brother Thomas More Page

Let Us Possess Ourselves in Patience

93　Take from us, O God, all tediousness of spirit, all
　　impatience and unquietness.　Let us possess
　　ourselves in patience, through Jesus Christ our
　　Lord.

　　　　　　　　Jeremy Taylor

Perfect Silence

94　I see no way of truthfully praising you
　　For except silence you do not put on any other
　　　　　ornament.
　　Your true praise consists in perfect silence
　　Your worship is no outer act,
　　And union with you is being nothing myself.
　　But, if, like one whose mind is crazed
　　And wildly babbles,
　　I sing your praise:
　　Bear with it,
　　O dear Mother.

　　　　　　　　Dnyanadev's prayer from his
　　　　　　　　commentary on the
　　　　　　　　Bhagavad Gita

Stillness

95   Give unto us, O Lord, that quietness of mind in
which we can hear you speaking to us.

Anonymous

His Earthly Life in Silence

96   Let us adore Jesus in our hearts, who spent thirty
years out of thirty-three in silence; who began his
public life by spending forty days in silence; who
often retired alone to spend the night on a
mountain in silence. He who spoke with
authority, now spends his earthly life in silence.
Let us adore Jesus in the eucharistic silence.

Mother Teresa of Calcutta

Alone

97   Grant me the ability to be alone;
may it be my custom to go outdoors each day
among the trees and grasses,
among all growing things,
and there may I be alone,
to talk with the one
that I belong to.

Rabbi Nachman of Bratzlav

Just to Be

98 Just to be is a blessing.
    Just to live is holy.

                    Rabbi Abraham Heschel

In Quiet

99 Shut the eyes that flame and hush the heart that
            burns:
    In quiet we may hear the old primeval cry:
    God gives wisdom to the spirit that upturns:
    Let us adore now, you and I.

                    George Russell

The True Mosque

100 Fools laud and magnify the mosque
    While they oppress the holy ones of heart.
    But the former is mere form; the latter, spirit and
            truth.

    The only true mosque
    Is the one in the hearts of saints.

                    Rúmí

Sight

101 You see me through my own eyes, Lord,
but I do not recognize you;
If I could, I would see you
    through yours.
What lips leave unspoken,
fingers fail to touch,
eyes will not see. . . .
I'm in the palm of your hand, Lord,
though thou art beyond my reach.

Sweet Lord, let me dissolve completely
into your heart's prayer,
silent prayer, lovely prayer,
joyous adoring contemplative
    communion as prayer.

Lama Surya Das

I Believe

102 I believe in the sun even when it is not shining.
I believe in love even when feeling it not.
I believe in God even when he is silent.

Jewish prayer

Prayer for the Day of Atonement

103　May you be answered in Heaven in full response
of loving mercy.

May your imploring prayers be answered, your
entreaty accepted and your appeal received with
favor.

May the Lord our God open to you and all Israel:

The Gates of Prayer
The Gates of Quietude
The Gates of Torah.

May God remove from among you envy,
contention, and hatred.

May God fulfill for you the biblical word, "The
Lord God of your fathers multiply you a
thousandfold and bless you as promised you."

May God inscribe you for good in the book of
life.

May this be God's will and let us say, Amen.

Sephardic Jewish prayer

The Collect for Purity

104 Almighty God, unto whom all hearts be open, all
desires known, and from whom no secrets are
hid;

Cleanse the thoughts of our hearts by the
inspiration of your holy Spirit,
That we may perfectly love you, and worthily
magnify your holy Name;
Through Christ our Lord.
Amen.

> Leofric, *The Book of Common
> Prayer*, 1050

Calm Hope of the Coptic Liturgy

105 Lord our God, great, eternal, wonderful in glory,
Who keeps covenant and promises for those that
love you with their whole heart;
Who are the Life of all, the Help of those that
flee to you, the Hope of those who cry unto you;
Cleanse us from our sins, secret and open, and
from every thought displeasing to your goodness—
Cleanse our bodies and souls, our hearts and
consciences,
That with a pure heart and a clear soul, with
perfect love and calm hope, we may venture
confidently and fearlessly to pray to you.

> From a prayer in the liturgy of
> Saint Basil

Litany

106 *The priest:*
    Almighty, everlasting God.
    The people sing:
    Have mercy upon us.
    The priest:
    O Lord, hear our prayer.

> from the Rite of the
> Swedish Church

---

107   *O God, make us children of
    quietness, and heirs of peace.*

> Saint Clement

Intimacy With God

To Know God and Be Transformed

✦

Prayers for Wisdom, Knowledge, Discernment,
and Illumination

✦

Help Thou My Unbelief

✦

Repentance Before the Creator

✦

Divine Consolation

To Know God
and Be Transformed

Prayer purifies; it is a self-preached sermon.
—Jean Paul

Change

108   My God I'm here before thee
I crumble into nothing before thee
I adore thy greatness
My need is immense
Have pity on me
Let thy spirit dwell in me
Let the Holy Spirit live in me
The love of the Father and the Son
So that I may love thee and thou me.

Raissa Maritain

At All Times and Places

109   Creator, where shall I find you?
All hidden and exalted is your place.
And where shall I not find you?
Full of your glory is the infinite space.

I have sought your nearness,
with all my heart I called you
and going out to meet you
I found you coming to meet me.

Judah Halevi

Rábi'a's Prayer

110   All-knowing Lord,
Make this world's goods the portion of your foes
And Paradise your followers' reward.
But as for me, remote from these and those
   I stand, for ever free.
Losing both worlds, I count the loss as light
If for one instant I may be your friend;
Content I'd take from you a beggar's plight—
From you my true content, wealth without end,
   Yourself your gift to me.

Islamic woman mystic

Day by Day

111 Thanks be to you,
     Lord Jesus Christ,
     for all the benefits
     that you have won for us,
     for all the pains and insults
     that you have borne for us.
     O most merciful Redeemer,
     Friend and Brother,
     may we know you more clearly,
     love you more dearly,
     follow you more nearly,
     day by day.

Richard of Chichester

Please

112 O Lord, that lends me life,
     Lend me a heart replete with thankfulness.

William Shakespeare

To Know You

113 O Lord, you have searched me, and known me.
You understand my thought afar off.
You compass my path and my lying down,
And are acquainted with all my ways;
For there is not a word in my tongue, but lo
You know it altogether.

O you who know me so utterly, help me to
know you
a little.

Arthur Stanley Fisher

Yet

114 Lord, I am not yet willing for you to have your
way with me.

But I am willing to be made willing.

F. B. Meyer

After Brother Lawrence

115 Thou art the hammer, Lord,
     And I am a nail;
     I'm fresh wheat,
     And thou art the flail.

     I'm an uncarved block of stone
        in your hands, Lord:
           Do with me what you will.

                 Lama Surya Das

Why

116 God in heaven,
     Let me really feel my nothingness,
     Not in order to despair over it,
     But in order to feel the more powerfully
     The greatness of your goodness.

                 Søren Kierkegaard

Make Me . . .

117   O God, our true life, to know you is life, to
serve you is freedom, to enjoy you is a kingdom,
to praise you is the joy and happiness of the soul.
I praise and bless and adore you, I worship you,
I glorify you. I give thanks to you for your great
glory. I humbly beg you to live with me, to
reign in me, to make this heart of mine a holy
temple, a fit habitation for your divine majesty.

Saint Augustine

Into Thy Hands

118   Father, into thy hands I commend my spirit.

Jesus of Nazareth,
while on the cross (Luke 23:46)

Come, O Lord

119   Come, O Lord, in much mercy down into my
soul, and take possession and dwell there. A
homely mansion, I confess, for so glorious a
majesty, but one such as you are fitting up for
the reception of you, by holy and fervent desires
of your own inspiring.

Enter then, and adorn, and make it such as you
can inhabit, since it is the work of your hands.
Give me your own self, without which, though
you were to give me all that ever you have
made, yet could not my desires be satisfied.

Let my soul ever seek you, and let me persist in
seeking, till I have found, and am in full
possession of you.

Amen.

Saint Augustine

Lest Our Peace Be Broken

120 Grant us, O Lord, the blessing of those whose
minds are stayed upon you, so that we may be
kept in perfect peace—a peace which cannot be
broken. Let not our minds rest upon any
creature, but only in the Creator: not upon
goods, things, houses, lands, inventions of
vanities or foolish fashions, lest our peace be
broken and we become cross and brittle and
given over to envy.

From all such, deliver us, O God,
and grant us your peace.

George Fox

All

121 God, of your goodness give me Yourself
for You are sufficient for me.

I cannot properly ask anything less,
to be worthy of You.

If I were to ask anything less, I should
always be in want.

In You alone do I have all.

Julian of Norwich

Conform My Will to Yours

122 O Lord, let me not henceforth desire health or
life, except to spend them for you, with you,
and in you.

You alone know what is good for me; do,
therefore, what seems best to you. Give to me,
or take from me; conform my will to yours; and
grant that, with humble and perfect submission,
and in holy confidence, I may receive the orders
of your eternal providence; and may equally
adore all that comes to me from you.

Blaise Pascal

Ash Wednesday

123   Give me grace, O my Father, to be utterly
ashamed of my own reluctance.

Rouse me from sloth and coldness, and make
me desire you with my whole heart.

Teach me to love meditation, sacred reading,
and prayer.

Teach me to love that which must engage my
mind for all eternity.

John Henry Newman

Think Through Me

124   Holy Spirit
think through me
till your ideas
are my ideas.

Amy Carmichael

Write Your Name

125   Write your blessed Name, O Lord,
      upon my heart, there to remain so indelibly
          engraved,
      that no prosperity, no adversity
      will ever move me from your love.

      Be to me a strong tower of defense,
      a comforter in tribulation,
      a deliverer in distress,
      a very present help in trouble,
      and a guide to heaven through the many
          temptations
      and dangers of this life.

                          Thomas à Kempis

Metamorphosis

126   Dear Lord and Father of mankind . . .
      Re-clothe us in our rightful mind . . .
      And let our ordered lives confess
      The beauty of your peace.

                          John Greenleaf Whittier

Prayers for Wisdom, Knowledge, Discernment, and Illumination

Reason is a light God has kindled in the soul.
—Aristotle

Help me never to use my reason against the Truth.
—Jewish prayer

To the Deity Asclepios

127   Adoring your goodness,
       we make this our only prayer . . .
       That you would be willing to keep us all our lives
       In the love of your knowledge.

Attributed to Apuleius

To Seek Wisely

128   God of all goodness, grant us to desire ardently,
to seek wisely, to know surely,
and to accomplish perfectly your holy will,
for the glory of your name.

Saint Thomas Aquinas

Wish for Wisdom

129   Wisdom of serpent be thine,
Wisdom of raven be thine,
   Wisdom of valiant eagle.

Voice of swan be thine,
Voice of honey be thine,
   Voice of the son of the stars.

Bounty of sea be thine,
Bounty of land be thine,
   Bounty of the Father of heaven.

Celtic blessing

Queen of Wisdom

130   Hail, Queen Wisdom! May the Lord preserve you
   with your sister holy pure Simplicity!
O lady holy Poverty, may the Lord save you
   with your sister holy Humility!

O lady holy Charity, may the Lord save you
    with your sister holy Obedience!
O all you most holy virtues,
    may the Lord save you all,
    from Whom you come and proceed.

Saint Francis of Assisi

The Way

131   O Wisdom, that came out of the mouth
    of the Most High,
    Reaching from one end to another, mightily
    and sweetly ordering all things:

Come to teach us the way of understanding.

Ancient Christian collect

A Prayer Before Praying

132   May the words of my mouth
    And the meditation of my heart
    Be acceptable in your sight
    O Lord, my strength and my redeemer.

Psalm 19:14

Let Us See

133   Almighty and everliving God, you are beyond
the grasp of our highest thought, but within the
reach of our frailest trust:

Come in the beauty of the morning's light and
reveal yourself to us. Enrich us out of the
heritage of seers and scholars and saints into
whose faith and labors we have entered, and
quicken us to new insights for our time; that we
may be possessors of the truth of many
yesterdays, partakers of your thoughts for today,
and creators with you of a better tomorrow;
through Jesus Christ, the Lord of the ages.

Henry Sloane Coffin

Compass

134   O my God, my soul is a ship
adrift in the seas of her own will,
where there is no shelter from you except in you.

Appoint for her, O God, in the name of God,
her course
and its harbor.

Muslim prayer

Sunnah for Guidance

135   O Allah,
    if in your knowledge this matter is good for my
        faith,
    for my livelihood and for the outcome of my
        affairs,
    then decide it for me and make it easy for me
        and bless me therein;
    but if in your knowledge this matter is bad for
        my faith
    for my livelihood and for the outcome of my
        affairs,
    then turn it away from me, and turn me away
        therefrom,
    and decide for me the good wherever it be,
    and cause me to be pleased therewith.

Muhammad

Illumination

136   Almighty and everlasting God, who has made
known the incarnation of your word by the
testimony of a glorious star, which when the wise
men beheld, they adored your majesty with gifts;
Grant that the star of your righteousness may
always appear in our hearts, and our treasure
consist in giving thanks to you.

Gelasian Sacramentary,
collect for Christmas

Radiant Is the World Soul

137 Radiant is the world soul,
Full of splendor and beauty,
Full of life,
Of souls hidden,
Of treasures of the holy spirit,
Of fountains of strength,
Of greatness and beauty.
Proudly I ascend
Toward the heights of the world soul
That gives life to the universe.
How majestic the vision,
Come, enjoy,
Come, find peace,
Embrace delight,
Taste and see that God is good.
Why spend your substance on what does not
    nourish?
And your labor on what cannot satisfy?
Listen to me, and you will enjoy what is good,
And find delight in what is truly precious.

Rabbi Abraham Isaac Kook

Light

138   O God, give me light in my heart
and light in my tongue
and light in my hearing
and light in my sight
and light in my feeling
and light in all my body
and light before me
and light behind me.

Give me, I pray Thee,
light on my right hand
and light on my left hand
and light above me
and light beneath me,
O Lord, increase light within me
and give me light
and illuminate me.

Attributed to Muhammad

Come, My Light

139   Come, my light, and illuminate my darkness.
Come my life, and revive me from death.
Come my physician, and heal my wounds.
Come, flame of divine love, and burn up the
thorns of my misdeeds,
kindling my heart with the flame of your love.
Come, my God, sit upon the throne of my heart
and reign there.
For you alone are my God and my Lord.

Saint Dimitri of Rostov

Discern With Me

140   Grant me, O Lord, to know what I ought to
know, to love what I ought to love, to praise
what delights you most, to value what is precious
in your sight, to hate what is offensive to you.

Do not allow me to judge according to the sight
of my eyes, nor to pass sentence according to the
hearing of the ears of ignorant men; but to
discern with a true judgment between things
visible and spiritual, and above all things, always
to inquire what is the good pleasure of your will.

Thomas à Kempis

The Serenity Prayer

141   God, grant me the serenity
to accept the things I cannot change
the courage to change the things I can
and the wisdom to know the difference.

Attributed to Reinhold Niebuhr

From Doubts Impossible to Be Solved

142   O Lord, my Maker and Protector, who hast graciously sent me into this world to work out my salvation, enable me to drive from me all such unquiet and perplexing thoughts as may mislead or hinder me in the practice of those duties which Thou hast required.

When I behold the works of thy hands, and consider the course of thy providence, give me grace always to remember that thy thoughts are not my thoughts, nor thy ways my ways.

And while it shall please Thee to continue me in this world, where much is to be done, and little to be known, teach me by thy Holy Spirit, to withdraw my mind from unprofitable and dangerous enquiries, from difficulties vainly curious, and doubts impossible to be solved.

Let me rejoice in the light which Thou hast imparted, let me serve Thee with active zeal and humble confidence, and wait with patient expectation for the time in which the soul which Thou receivest shall be satisfied with knowledge. Grant this, O Lord, for Jesus Christ's sake.

Samuel Johnson

Eyes to See

143   O gracious and holy Father,
       Give us wisdom to perceive you,
       intelligence to understand you,
       diligence to seek you,
       patience to wait for you,
       eyes to see you,
       a heart to meditate on you,
       and a life to proclaim you,
       through the power of the spirit of Jesus Christ
       our Lord.

                    Saint Benedict

The Sarum Primer Prayer

144   God be in my head
       and in my understanding;
       God be in my eyes
       and in my looking;
       God be in my mouth
       and in my speaking;
       God be in my heart
       and in my thinking;
       God be at my end
       and at my departing.

                         Private service book,
                         Clare College, Cambridge

Self-Knowing

145 Janārdan is the Lord of the three worlds.
      He opened an account with me.
  He gave me "I AM HE" as his bond.
      I reverently accepted it.
  I will collect the revenue of Self-knowledge
      And I will send it to my *suāmi.*

Eknath

Good Morning to You, God, I Am Learning

146 The heavens are wide, exceedingly wide.
  The earth is wide, very, very wide.
  We have lifted it and taken it away.
  We have lifted it and brought it back.
  From time immemorial,
  The God of old bids us all
  Abide by his injunctions.
  Then shall we get whatever we want,
  Be it white or red.
  It is God, the Creator, the Gracious One.
  Good morning to you, God.
  Good morning.
  I am learning, let me succeed.

Drum poem from the Akan
people of Ghana

Help Thou My Unbelief

The wish to pray is a prayer in itself
—Source unknown

❦

Divine Grace

147   Lord, take my heart, for I cannot give it to you.
And when you have it, keep it,
For I would not take it from you.
And save me
in spite of myself
for Christ's sake.

François Fénelon

◆

148   Lord, I believe.
Help Thou my unbelief.

Mark 9:24

Freedom

149   May we not worry but believe in thee, our
      Great Parent.

                    Bunjiro Kawate

---

150   *Thy will be done, though in my*
      own undoing.

                    Sir Thomas Browne

Even When

151   I will try to pray,
      even when I am afraid to face you and myself,
      even when I keep falling asleep,
      or feel as though I am going around in circles,
      even when it seems that nothing is happening. . . .

      Let me see myself in the light of your mercy
      and choose you.

                    Henri Nouwen

The Mul Mantra . . .

152   There is but one God;
Eternal Truth is his name.
Creator of all things,
All-pervading spirit,
Fearless and without hatred,
Timeless and formless,
Beyond birth and death,
Self-existent,
Known through his grace.

. . . and the Japji Sahib

God is not to be comprehended by human
    thought,
    Though we may try it a hundred thousand
       times.
Outward silence cannot still the mind's search
    for truth,
    Though we absorb ourselves in meditation
       long and deep.
Our hunger for God can never be satisfied,
    Even if we acquire everything the universe has
       to offer.
If we increase our wisdom beyond measure,
    It is still not enough.
How, then, can we come to know the truth?
How can the veil of falsehood be torn asunder?
By following God's will, O Nanak,
Which is written within our hearts.

Opening words of Sikh devotions

Teach Us, O Lord

153   Teach us, O Lord, to fear you without being
          afraid;
      to fear you in love that we may love you
          without fear.

Christina Rossetti

✦

154   Sometimes
      I go about pitying myself
      While I am carried by
      The wind
      Across the sky.

Chippewa song

✦

155   Make that possible to me, O Lord, by grace,
      which appears impossible to me by nature.

Thomas à Kempis

Teach Me

156   Teach me to seek thee, and reveal thyself to me
       when I seek thee, for I cannot seek thee except
       thou teach me, nor find thee, except thou reveal
       thyself.

Saint Anselm

You Have Pierced My Heart

157   Not with doubts but with a sure consciousness,
       do I love you, Lord. You have pierced my heart
       with your words, and I have loved you.

Saint Augustine

---

158   *Unto you, highest angels, I offer*
       sacrifice and prayer, with thought,
       with word, with action, with my
       being—with the very life of my
       body.

The Avesta

Repentance Before the Creator

Great is the power of teshuvah *(repentance), for it brings healing to the world. Even if only one person does* teshuvah, *both that one and the entire world are forgiven.*
—*Babylonian Talmud*

Who has repented travels toward God.
—*Theophan*

Rest Your Burdens on Him

159   What use this rush, this hurry
This burden of earthly duties?

God's purposes stand firm,
And you, his little one,
Need one thing only—

Trust that he is able and willing
to satisfy your needs.
Rest your burdens on him,
And you, his little one,
May play in safety by him.

This is the essence of it all—
God is,
God loves you,
God carries all your burdens.

Tukârâm

I Turn

160 O immeasurable love!
O gentle love!
Eternal fire!
You are that fire ever blazing,
O high eternal Trinity!
You are direct
without any twisting,
genuine
without any duplicity,
open
without any pretense.
Turn the eye of your mercy on your creatures.
I know that mercy is your hallmark,
and no matter where I turn
I find nothing but your mercy.

Saint Catherine of Siena

Thy Mercy to Me Is Thy Healing

161   Thy Name is my healing, O my God, and
      remembrance of Thee is my remedy. Nearness
      to Thee is my hope, and love for Thee is my
      companion. Thy mercy to me is my healing
      and my succor in both this world and the world
      to come. Thou, verily, art the All-Bountiful, the
      All-Knowing, the All-Wise.

                    Bahá'u'lláh

Hope in Him

162   The favors of the Lord are not exhausted,
      his mercies are not spent;
      They are renewed each morning,
      so great is his faithfulness.
      My portion is the Lord, says my soul;
      therefore I will hope in him.

                    Lamentations 3:22–24

"God Is Good"

163 *"Gott ist gut"*

> Carved into a barracks wall at
> Theresienstadt concentration
> camp during World War II

Repose

164 You have made us for yourself, and our hearts
are restless, until they rest in you.

> Saint Augustine

Surrender

165 Lord, I trust to thee, who sendest all these
sorrows upon me, to take them off again.

> John Kettlewell

Desire

166 O Lord our God, grant us grace
     to desire you with our whole heart,
     that so desiring we may seek and find you,
     and so finding you, may love you,
     and loving you, may hate those sins
     from which you have redeemed us.

            Saint Anselm

Pardon

167 O Lord, be gracious unto us! In all that we hear
     or see, in all that we say or do, be gracious unto
     us. I ask pardon of the Great God. I ask
     pardon at the sunset, when every sinner turns to
     Him. Now and for ever I ask pardon of God.
     O Lord, cover us from our sins, guard our
     children and protect our weaker friends.

                 A Bedouin camel-driver's
                 prayer at sunset

Repentance

168 May I,
   who though experiencing impermanence
      still grasp at permanence,
   And though having arrived at the gate of old age,
      am still proud of my youth
   And all sentient beings with as wrong notions as I
   Receive the blessings of developing the feeling of
      impermanence.

May I,
   who adhere to the three Refuges,
      but have little trust in my heart,
   And know the three trainings,
      but have cast them aside by neglecting their
      application,
   And all sentient beings as cowardly as I
   Receive the blessings of stable, irreversible faith.

May I,
   who am proud of my development of Bodhicitta
      but have yet to give birth to it
   And who have learned the path of the six perfections
      but am still conceited
   And all sentient beings with as narrow attitudes as I
   Receive the blessings of practicing
      the supreme Bodhicitta.

> From the nineteenth-century
> confession prayer of a
> Tibetan Buddhist lama

Our Brokenness

169   Grandfather,
      Look at our brokenness.

      We know that in all creation
      Only the human family
      Has strayed from the Sacred Way.

      We know that we are the ones
      Who are divided
      And we are the ones
      Who must come back together
      To walk in the Sacred Way.

      Grandfather,
      Sacred One,
      Teach us love, compassion, and honor
      That we may heal the Earth
      And heal each other.

                    Ojibway prayer

Trespass

170   I offer you prayers for all whom I have grieved,
      vexed and oppressed, by word or deed,
      knowingly or unknowingly, that you might
      equally forgive all of us our sins, and all of us
      our offenses against each other.

                    Thomas à Kempis

For Forgiveness

171   All that we ought to have thought
     and have not thought,
  All that we ought to have said
     and have not said,
  All that we ought to have done
     and have not done;

  All that we ought not to have thought
     and yet have thought,
  All that we ought not to have spoken
     and yet have spoken,
  All that we ought not to have done
     and yet have done:

  For thoughts, words and works, we pray,
     O God,
     for forgiveness.
  And repent with penance.

> The Zendavesta, ascribed to
> Zoroaster

Plenteous

172   You, Lord, are good, and ready to forgive
    And plenteous in mercy to all who call upon you.

Psalm 86:5

Humanity

173   Teach us, Lord, to accept our limitations.
It is of great advantage
that we shall know our place,
and not imagine that the whole universe
exists for us alone.

Maimonides

---

174   *He who knows his sins is much*
greater than he who makes
someone rise from the dead.

Isaac of Nineveh

Job's Final Words

175   In dust and ashes, I repent.

Job 42:6

Love

176   I have sinned against the Lord
      Have mercy on me!

      In whatever direction I turn
      I find unutterable love.
      So we can never be excused for not loving you,
      for it is you alone,
      God and human,
      who loved me without my having loved you,
      for I did not exist
      and you made me. . . .

                Saint Catherine of Siena

Prayer for Purity

177   Great Ulu, who kills and saves,
      I implore you to cleanse my household
          of all defilement.
      If I have spoken it with my mouth,
      Or seen it with my eyes,
      Or if I have heard it with my ears,
      Or stepped on it with my foot,
      Or if it has come through my children,
      Or my friends, or kinsfolk,
      Let it follow these leaves.

                Ibo woman's prayer

Good

178   King Zeus, grant us the good whether we pray
for it or not, but evil keep from us though we
pray for it.

Plato

The God of All Mercy

179   Almighty and everlasting God, who hates
nothing that you have made, and forgives the
sins of all those who are penitent: Create and
make in us new and contrite hearts, that we
worthily lamenting our sins, and acknowledging
our wretchedness, may obtain of you, the God
of all mercy, perfect remission and forgiveness,
through Jesus Christ our Lord.

From *The Book of Common Prayer*
Ash Wednesday service

Turn to Me

180   My child, I am the Lord who gives strength in
the day of troubles.

Come to me when it is not well with you.

For the thing that most of all hinders my
consolation to you

Is that you are too slow in turning yourself unto
prayer.

Thomas à Kempis

Sins I Have So Labored to Hide

181   Forgive me O Lord, O Lord forgive me my sins,
the sins of my youth, and my present sins, the
sins that my parents cast upon me, original sin,
and the sins that I cast upon my children, in an
ill example; actual sins, sins which are manifest
to all the world, and sins which I have so labored
to hide from the world that now they are hid
from my own conscience, and my own memory.

Forgive me my crying sins, and my whispering
sins. Let me be but so blessed, and I shall envy
no man's blessedness.

John Donne

For Loving Correction

182   Have mercy upon us, O Lord, have mercy upon
us, while you hasten not to consume us in our
utmost misery, but to make us free by your
loving mercy. Set yourself not to mark what is
done amiss but to pardon our iniquities.

O Lord, may we feel your hand a hand that
heals and does not wound, that cherishes and
does not strike, that you may so afflict us in this
present life that you save us from punishment in
the life to come.

With a father's pity correct your servants, but
cast them not away; teach them but confound
them not. Of your great goodness give to all
people peace without sin in their days . . .

Mozarabic Liturgy

Prayer of Eknāth

183   I am a great sinner, O Cloud-of-Mercy!
Take care of me, one lowly in heart.
Again and again, moment after moment,
I place my head at your feet.

I will use my body for a wave offering
Over your feet.
I am your servant.
Do not disappoint me.

Sixteenth-century Hindu prayer

184
You, Lord, are good, and ready to
forgive, and plenteous in mercy to
all who call upon you.

Psalm 86:5

The Shoulders Get Tired of Carrying Sins

185
Light, thou angel of light,
Thou, mighty one of the road
Which cometh from Jerusalem!
The shoulders get tired of carrying sins,
Oh, help us with this thy lamb,
So that it will be strong and fat,
So that we shall succeed through it,
The day when we bring back thy daughter.

South African Zionist Nazarite
hymn for the sacrifice of
a blessing ox

The Confession

186   Almighty God, our heavenly Father,
we have sinned against you and against our
fellow men,
in thought and word and deed,
through negligence, through weakness,
through our own deliberate fault.
We are truly sorry,
and repent of all our sins.
For the sake of your son Jesus Christ, who died
for us,
forgive us all that is past;
and grant that we may serve you in newness of
life
to the glory of your name.

> The Church of England's
> Alternative Service Book

Prayer of Saint Nerses

187   Beholder of all, I have sinned against you, in
thought, word, and deed;
Wipe out the record of my offenses, and write
my name in the Book of Life.
Have mercy upon your creatures, and upon me,
a manifold sinner.

> From the Ancient Armenian
> Book of Office and Divine Liturgy

Reverse Confession

188   Father, as I am here,
I have not stolen the goods of another,
I have not taken the good of another
Without recompense;
I have not set my heart after the goods of
another;
All men are good in my eyes.
God, it is indeed you
Who settles the difference
Between us who are men.

Zande people of Sudan

Bless the One Who Can Confess

189   May the everlasting Father Himself take you
In his own generous clasp
In his own generous arm.

From the *Carmina Gadelica*

Recovery

190   I bless you, O Lord,
       for you have granted me
       the power to repent from my sins
       and have shown to me myriad occasions
       to return from my malice.
       I bless you, O Lord,
       for though I am powerless,
       yet you strengthen my weakness
       and you suffer me not to fall utterly,
       but straightway
       you stretch forth from above
       your helping hand
       and bring me back unto yourself.

Saint Basil the Great

For Growth in Grace

191   Grant, O our God, that we may know you, love
       you, and rejoice in you; and if in this life we
       cannot do these things fully, grant that we may
       at the least progress in them from day to day,
       for Christ's sake.

Saint Anselm

The Jesus Prayer

192 Lord Jesus Christ, Son of God, have mercy on
me, a sinner.

Used for meditation in the
Eastern Orthodox church

The Tax Collector's Petition

193 God, be merciful to me, a sinner.

Luke 18:13

Peace I Give Unto You

194 Peace I leave with you,
my peace I give unto you:
not as the world gives,
give I unto you.
Let not your heart be troubled,
neither let it be afraid.

John 14:27

Divine Consolation

Call upon God, saying, "Things overwhelm me: come to my help."
—Noah the Muslim

The sure relief of prayer.
—William Wordsworth

Beauty

195 Today I will walk out, today everything evil will
leave me, I will be as I was before. I will have a
cool breeze over me, I will travel with a light body.
I will be happy forever, nothing will hinder me.
I walk with beauty before me, I walk with
beauty behind me,
I walk with beauty above me,
I walk with beauty all around me, my words
will be beautiful.

Navajo prayer

Counting Our Blessings:
A Prayer of Thanksgiving

196   Thank you, Lord,
     for this day,
     for this our life,
     for all your graces and delights;
     for this our bread,
     for this our breath, for this our wine,
     for wholeness, health and peace of mind;
     for these fruitful fields, forests
        and sparkling streams,
     for these mountains reflected
        in calm, clear lakes;
     for this air made fragrant by wildflowers
        and birdsong,
     for all your children gathered here
     for this eternal instant
        in your name,

     in this your spirit,
     in this your light
        in this our life,
     in this your temple
     in this house,
     in this your heart and soul,
     your body and mind
     to which we are
        far nearer
        than we know—

for all is well
and all shall be well
in this
            your perfect
                            world.

Amen.

Lama Surya Das

I Cannot Repay Such Mercy

197 The sins of my entire life,
         by which I have so often offended you,
     my God, weigh me down like a mountain
         of my own making.
     I wonder, "What will be the end
         of all this?"
     Yet, I do not lose hope.

     I cannot bear this alone;
         I know I am weak.
     But your strength will keep me from falling.
     The prayers of others will
         uphold me in my time of need.
     I cannot repay such mercy;
         to offer my life is only right.

                John Ri

Inclined

198 O Father,
lean lovingly over your poor small creature,
cover her with your shadow,
seeing in her only
the Beloved in whom you are well pleased.

Blessed Elizabeth of the Trinity

Consolation

199 Let nothing disturb you,
Let nothing dismay you.
All things pass.
God never changes.
Patience attains
all that it strives for.
He who has God
finds he lacks nothing.
God alone suffices.

Saint Teresa of Avila

Unfailing

200   Conceive the Soul as a fountain,
And these created things as rivers:
While the Fountain flows, the rivers run from it.

Put grief out of your mind,
And drink of this River-water.
Do not think of the Water failing—

For this Water is without end.

Rúmí

All Our Relations

For Our Families, Homes, and
Loved Ones

✦

Prayers by and for Children

✦

Intercessions for Healing and Comfort

✦

Petitions for Ourselves and Others

For Our Families, Homes, and Loved Ones

Walk together, talk together, O you people of the earth,
and then, only then, can you have peace.
—Vedic teaching

It is godlike for mortal to assist mortal.
—Pliny the Elder

If you seek yourself, you will find yourself.
And that to your own ruin.
—Thomas à Kempis

Tenth-Century Celtic Wish

201   I wish, O Son of the living God, ancient eternal King, for a secret hut in the wilderness that it may be my dwelling.

A very blue shallow well to be beside it, a clear pool for washing away sins through the grace of the Holy Spirit.

A beautiful wood close by around it on every side, for the nurture of many-voiced birds, to shelter and hide it.

Facing the south for warmth, a little stream across its enclosure, a choice ground with abundant bounties which would be good for every plant.

A few wise disciples, I will tell their number, humble and obedient, to pray to the King:

Four threes, three fours, fit for every need, two sixes in the church both south and north.

Six couples in addition to me myself, praying through the long ages to the King who moves the sun.

A lovely church decked with linen, a dwelling for God of Heaven; then, bright candles over the holy white Scriptures.

One room to go to for the care of the body, without wantonness, without voluptuousness, without meditation of evil.

This is the housekeeping I would undertake, I would choose it without concealing: fragrant fresh leeks, hens, speckled salmon, bees.

My fill of clothing and of food from the King of good fame, and for me to be sitting for a while praying to God in every place.

Manchán of Liath

Inhabit This Dwelling

202 Almighty and everlasting God, be present to our duties, and grant the protection of your presence to all who dwell in this house; that you may be known to be the Defender of your family, and the Inhabitant of this dwelling.

Gelasian Sacramentary

A True Home

203   May obedience conquer disobedience within
      this house,
and may peace triumph over discord here,
and generous giving over avarice,
reverence over contempt,
speech with truthful words over lying utterance;
may the righteous order gain the victory
over the demon of the lie.

Zoroastrian prayer

A Gate for God

204   O God, make the door of this house
wide enough to receive all who need
human love and fellowship;
narrow enough to shut out all envy, pride, and
strife.

Make its threshold smooth enough to be no
stumbling-block to children, nor to straying
feet, but rugged and strong enough to turn back
the tempter's power.

God make the door of this house the gateway to
your eternal kingdom.

Inscription at Saint Stephen's
Church, Walbrook, London

Prayer for Entering a New House

205   My father built,
And his father built,
And I have built.
Ancestors: Leave me to live here in success,
Let me sleep in comfort,
And have children.
There is food for you.

Nyoro people of Uganda

For Absent Friends

206   O Lord God Almighty, who dwells in love, and
out of whose gift it comes that the bond of
affection is not cut by bodily absence, and that
the flame of sacred love is not extinguished by
parting, but rather increased by longing
remembrance;
we pray and beseech you that tireless affection
may remain in us true and pure, always recalling
the absent to loving memory, and keeping
present in our hearts those who are far away.

Be pleased, O Lord, to prosper the course of
your servants, to keep and defend them from all
the snares of the enemy.

Mozarabic Book of Orders

Honor to Those Before Us

207   O God, let my prayer reach all our forefathers
Who are in your arms.

Mende people of Sierra Leone

Families

208   For our absent loved ones we implore your
loving-kindness. Keep them in life, keep them
in glowing honor; and for us, grant that we
remain worthy of their love. . . . And grant us
courage to endure lesser ills unshaken, and to
accept death, loss, and disappointment as it
were straws upon the tide of life.

Robert Louis Stevenson

O My Father and Mother

209   O God my Father and Mother,
       I have not listened to you
       Nor sung your praises.
       I have been ashamed of you
       And have thrown away what was for my good.
       I am my own destroyer.
       I am my own enemy, my own bitter foe.
       But you are an Ocean of Mercy.
       Take me safely to the other side.

                    Tukārâm

Marriage Blessing

210   The Lord sanctify and bless you,
       the Lord pour the riches of his grace upon you,
       that you may please him
       and live together in holy love
       to your lives' end.
       So be it.

                    John Knox

One Another

211   O God, out of all the world you let us find one
another and learn together the meaning of love.
Let us never fail to hold love precious. Let the
flame of it never waver or grow dim, but burn
in our hearts as an unwavering devotion and
shine through our eyes in gentleness and
understanding on which no shadow falls. . . .

Teach us to remember the little courtesies, to be
swift to speak the grateful and happy word, to
believe rejoicingly in each other's best, and to
face all life bravely because we face it with
united heart.

Walter Russell Bowie

May All Beings Be Happy

212   May all beings be happy
May all beings be free from suffering
May all beings be at peace.

The Dalai Lama

Prayers by and for Children

*Every time a baby is born, it brings with it the hope that
God is not yet disappointed with humanity.*
—Rabindranath Tagore

And a little child will lead them.
—Isaiah 11:6

The Great Worth of a Newborn Child

213   O Muumbi,
You who have created
All human beings,
You have conferred
A great benefit on us
By bringing us this child.

Kamba prayer from Kenya

A Prayer to a Mother, Mary

214   Radiant
mother of sacred healing!
you poured salve on the sobbing
wounds that Eve sculpted
to torment our souls.
For your salve is your son and you
wrecked death forever,
sculpturing life.

Pray for us to your child,
Mary, star of the sea.

O life-giving source and gladdening sign and
sweetness of all
delights that flow unfailing!

Pray for us to your child,
Mary, star of the sea.

Glorify the Father,
the Spirit and the Son.

Pray for us to your child,
Mary, star of the sea.

Saint Hildegard of Bingen

Descendants

215 Let us behave gently,
that we may die peacefully;
That our children may stretch out their hands
upon us in burial.

Yoruba prayer, Nigeria

Simplicity

216 O my Lord! O my Lord!

I am a child of tender years.
Nourish me from the breast of Thy mercy, train
me in the bosom of Thy love, educate me in the
school of Thy guidance and develop me under
the shadow of Thy bounty.

Deliver me from darkness, make me a brilliant
light; free me from unhappiness, make me a
flower of the rose garden; suffer me to become a
servant of Thy threshold and confer upon me
the disposition and nature of the righteous;
make me a cause of bounty to the human
world, and crown my head with the diadem of
eternal life.

Verily, Thou art the Powerful, the Mighty, the
Seer, the Hearer.

'Abdu'l-Bahá

Father-Mother God, Loving Me

217   Father-Mother God
loving me,
Guide my little feet
Up to Thee

        Author unknown

The Child's Evening Prayer

218   Now I lay me down to sleep,
I pray the Lord my soul to keep;
If I should die before I wake,
I pray the Lord my soul to take.

        New England Primer, eighteenth
        century, based on a manuscript
        from 1160 A.D.

Prayers for Young People

219   O God, since you often seem unreal and far
away, please make yourself real and near to me,
so that I may be what you would have me be
and act as you would have me act.

O God, please give me clarity of mind, so that
seeing other people in every situation as they
are, and not as confused by my own hopes and
fears, I may act according to your truth.

O God, help me to think before I speak or act,
so as to relate my speech and actions to an end
that is worthy and pleasing to you.

O God, make me brave and able to stand the
strain: teach me to understand that courage
does not lie so much in aggressiveness, as in
being patient—patient with myself, with other
people, and with the disagreeable situations that
duty requires me to face.

O God, guard me against the evils of hatred,
aversion, and resentment. As long as I harbor
these, all peace is gone; so help me to turn my
mind away from these deadly darkeners of the
heart.

O God, teach me the secret of true joy: give me
the grace to live in the present, not to be
overanxious about the future, to regard those
around me cheerfully but with affectionate
concern, and not to take myself too seriously.

Dom Aelred Graham

Child's Prayer of Thanks

220   Thank you, heavenly Father,
        for my bread,
        my dad and mother and my bed.
        Amen.

Anonymous

Small Things

221   Dear Father,
        Hear and bless
        Your beasts
        And singing birds:
        And guard with tenderness
        Small things
        That have no words.

Anonymous

Bedtime

222   Matthew, Mark, Luke, and John,
Bless the bed I lie upon.
Four corners to my bed,
Four angels round my head,
One to watch, and one to pray,
And two to bear my soul away.

Traditional

The Holy One Above Us

223   Blessing of green plants, blessing of forests:
Cedar, douglas fir, swordfern, salal bush
Blessing of fish and birds, blessing of mammals:
Salmon, eagle, cougar and mountain goat.

May all humankind likewise offer blessing:
Old woman, young woman, wise men and
foolish
Blessing of youthfulness, blessing of children
Big boys, little boys, big girls and little ones.

Bless the wisdom of the holy one above us;
Bless the truth of the holy one beneath us;
Bless the love of the holy one within us.

Chinook Psalter

Dutch Lullaby

224   *Ik ga slapen, ik ben moe,*
Sluit mijn oojes beide toe,
Heere, houd ook deze nacht,
Over mij getrouw de wacht.

Booze daad ik heb gedaan,
Ziehet Heere, toch niet aan,
Schoon mijn zonden vele zijn,
Maak om Jezus wil mij rein.

Weary now, I go to sleep,
Eyes both closed for slumber deep,
Lord wilt Thou, my constant friend,
Me—Thy child—this night defend.

Evil deeds that I have done,
Lord, do Thou not look upon,
Many though my sins may be,
Clean, for Jesus's sake, make me.

Traditional prayer of the Netherlands

From All Who Once Were Children

225   O God! Take this my prayer
And touch all unhappy children
Everywhere.

Anonymous

Delight

226   My lord is full of blessing.
       In his left hand he holds dancing plumes.
       With his right he summons me to dance with
           him.
       Oh, what sweet joy!

The Book of Songs (Chinese)

A Parent's Plea to the Creator

227   O God, you are great,
       You are the one who created me,
       I have no other.
       God, you are in the heavens,
       You are the only one:
       Now my child is sick,
       And you will grant me my desire.

Anuak people of Sudan

Prayer to Mother Mary

228 Dear Mary, thou didst see thy first-born Son
Go forth to die amidst the scorn of men
For whom he died.

Receive my first-born son into thy arms
And keep him by thee till I come for him.
Dear Mary, I have shared thy sorrow,
And soon shall share thy joy.

> Padraic Pearse, written for
> his mother before his execution

The Mother

229 I do not grudge them: Lord, I do not grudge
My two strong sons that I have seen go out
To break their strength and die, they and a few,
In bloody protest for a glorious thing;
They shall be spoken of among their people,
The generations shall remember them,
And call them blessed;
But I will speak their names to my own heart
In the long nights;
The little names that were familiar once
Round my dead hearth.
Lord, Thou are hard on mothers;
We suffer in their coming and their going;
And though I grudge them not, I weary, weary
Of the long sorrow—and yet I have my joy:
My sons were faithful, and they fought.

> Padraic Pearse

Intercessions for Healing and Comfort

*To clasp the hands in prayer
is the beginning of an uprising
against the disorder of the world.*
—Karl Barth

Two Ancient Prayers for Healing

230 *O God of Hosts,* who takes away all sickness and
infirmity by your mighty word: mercifully assist
your servant that, being set free from his
weakness and renewed in strength, he may
straightway recover his health and bless your
Holy Name.

O God, who out of your tender love gives
warning to the work of your hands: incline your
ear to our prayers and mercifully regard the
afflictions of your servant. Visit him with your
salvation and give him the help of your heavenly
grace.

Gelasian Sacramentary

After the Death of His Wife

233   O Lord, our heavenly Father, without whom all
purposes are frustrate, and efforts are vain, grant
me the assistance of your Holy Spirit, that I may
not sorrow as one without hope, but may now
return to the duties of my present state with
humble confidence in your protection, and so
govern my thoughts and actions, that neither
business may withdraw my mind from you, nor
idleness lay me open to vain imaginations; that
neither praise may fill me with pride, nor
censure with discontent; but that in the changes
of this life, I may fix my heart upon the reward
which you have promised to them that serve
you, and that whatever things are true, whatever
are pure, whatever are lovely, whatever are of
good report, wherein there is virtue, wherein
there is praise, I may think upon and do, and
obtain mercy and everlasting happiness. Grant
this, O Lord, for the sake of Jesus Christ.
Amen.

Samuel Johnson

Petitions for Ourselves and Others

Lord, make me
according to thy heart.
—Brother Lawrence

☙

Here, Lord, is my life. I place it on the altar today.
Use it as you will.
—Albert Schweitzer

☙

Grant Us to Be

234   Beloved God of the woods and streams,
grant us to be beautiful inwardly,
and all that we have of outer things
to be at peace with those within.
Counting only the wise to be truly rich,
increase to all who here abide
their stores of gold.

Plato

May Happiness Come

235   Hail, hail, hail.
May happiness come.
May meat come,
May corn come.
Just as the farmers work
And look forward to the reaping,
So may we sit again as we are sitting now.
May our enemies turn from us and go . . .
Lord return.

Ghanian prayer

The Will of God

236   The will of God be done by us,
The law of God be kept by us,
Our evil will controlled by us,
Our tongue in cheek be held by us,
Repentance timely made by us,
Christ's passion understood by us,
Each sinful crime be shunned by us,
Much on the *End* be mused by us,
And Death be blesséd found by us,
With Angel's music heard by us,
And God's high praises sung by us,
For ever and for aye.

Irish prayer

O Great Spirit . . .

237   whose voice I hear in the winds,
and whose breath puts life into all things,
hear my prayer!

I am small and weak,
I need your wisdom, and your strength.

Let me walk in beauty, and let me revere the red
and purple sunset.
Make my hands respect all things you have
made and my ears sharp to hear your voice.
Make me wise so that I may understand the
things you have taught my people.
Let me find the lessons you have hidden in
every leaf and rock.
I ask you for strength, not to be greater than
another, but to oppose my greatest enemy—
myself.

Make me always ready to come to you with
clean hands and straight eyes.
So when life fades, like the dwindling daylight,
my spirit may come to you without shame.

Native American prayer

Nayaz

238   Beloved Lord, Almighty God!
Through the rays of the Sun.
Through the waves of the air.
Through the All-pervading Life in space.
Purify and revivify me, and, I pray,
Heal my body, heart, and soul.
                    Amen.

Hazrat Inayat Khan

239   *Let those who have need of more*
ask for it humbly. And let those
who have need of less thank God.

The Rule of Saint Benedict

Mirror-Images

240   *What We Have Done . . .*

Have mercy on me, O Ishtar!
I have borne your yoke: give now consolation!
I have protected your splendor: let there be
good fortune and prosperity!
I have sought your light: let my brightness
shine!
I have turned toward your power: let there be
life and peace!
Speak and let the word be heard!
Prolong my days, bestow life:
Let me live, let me be perfect, let me behold
your divinity!

. . . And What God Has Done

O mighty Lord,
Since you are beneficent, I have turned
to your divinity!
Since you are compassionate, I have sought
for you!
Since you are merciful, I have taken my stand
before you!
Truly pity me and hearken to my cries!
O god and goddess,
Let me talk of your greatness, let me bow
in humility before you.

> Fragments of Babylonian tablet
> inscriptions

Radiance

241   You who are the true sun of the world, rising
and never going down, who by your most
wholesome appearing and sight nourishes and
makes joyful all things in heaven as on earth; we
beseech you mercifully and favorably to shine in
our hearts, that the night and darkness of sin,
and the mists of error on every side being driven
away, and with you shining in our hearts, we
may all our life long go without any stumbling
or offense, and may walk as in the daytime,
being pure and clean from the works of
darkness, and abounding in all good works
which you have prepared for us to walk in.

Desiderius Erasmus

Living Waters

242   Most great and glorious God, who has
appointed the rivers to hasten to the sea, make
the stream of our will perpetually to flow a
cheerful and impetuous course, bearing down all
impediments of affliction, pleasure, or self-
interest, till it plunge in the unfathomable ocean
of your love.

Charles Howe

Abba

243 Abba, Father, fulfil the office of your name
towards your servants.
Govern, protect, preserve, sanctify, guide,
console us; let us be so enkindled with love for
you that we may not be despised by you, O
most merciful Lord, most tender Father.

Gallican Sacramentary

---

244 *Lord, give me what you are
requiring of me.*

Saint Augustine

Chosen

245 O God, who has chosen the weak things of the
world to confound the mighty:
Shed forth continual day upon us who watch
for you,
That our lips might praise you,
Our life might bless you,
And our meditations glorify you.

Amen.

Sarum Breviary

---

246 *O eternal God: Let me, in spite of*
me, be of so much use to your
glory, that by your mercy to my
sin, other sinners may see how
much sin you can pardon.

John Donne

Prayer for Heavenly Waters

247   You, O Tsui-Goab!
Father of our fathers,
You, our father!
Let the thundercloud stream!
Let our flocks live!
Let us also live please.
I am so very weak indeed
From thirst,
From hunger!
Let me eat field fruits!
Are you not our father?
The father of the fathers,
You, Tsui-Goab.
That we may praise you!
That we may bless you!
You father of the fathers!
You, our Lord!
You, O Tsui-Goab!

Hottentot prayer against drought

---

248   *The things, good Lord, that we pray for,*
give us the grace to labor for.

Thomas More

All in All

249   Lord, I don't know what I ought to ask of you.
You alone know what I need.
You love me better than I know how to love
   myself.
O Father, give to me, your child, that which I
   don't know how to ask . . .
I would have no other wish than to do your
   will.
Teach me to pray.
Pray yourself in me.

François Fénelon

Necessity

250   Almighty and most merciful father
who sees all our miseries
and knows all our necessities,
Look down upon me, and pity me.

Have mercy on me, O God.
Years of infirmities oppress me,
terror and anxiety beset me.
Have mercy upon me, my Creator and
my Judge.

Samuel Johnson

The Holy Spirit

251   As the wind is thy symbol
       so forward our goings.
       As the dove
       so launch us heavenwards.
       As water
       so purify our spirits.
       As a cloud
       so abate our temptations.
       As dew
       so revive our languor.
       As fire
       so purge out our dross.

Christina Rossetti

---

252   *Grant us grace, Almighty Father,*
       so to pray as to deserve to be heard.

Jane Austen

Hear Us, Great Spirit

253   O our Father the Sky, hear us
     and make us bold.
  O our Mother the Earth, hear us
     and give us support.
  O Spirit of the East,
     send us your Wisdom.
  O Spirit of the South,
     may we walk your path of life.
  O Spirit of the West,
     may we always be ready for the long journey.
  O Spirit of the North, purify us
     with your cleansing winds.

Sioux prayer

---

254   *Create in me a clean heart,*
O my God, and renew a
right spirit within me.

Psalm 51:10

Supply Me

255   O Thou Whose face is the object of my
        adoration,
      Whose beauty is my sanctuary,
      Whose habitation is my goal,
      Whose praise is my hope,
      Whose providence is my companion,
      Whose love is the cause of my being,
      Whose mention is my solace,
      Whose nearness is my desire,
      Whose presence is my dearest wish and highest
        aspiration:

I entreat Thee not to withhold from me the
things Thou didst ordain for the chosen ones
among Thy servants.

Supply me, then, with the good of this world
and of the next.

Thou, truly, art the King of all men. There is
no God but Thee, the Ever-Forgiving, the Most
Generous.

Bahá'u'lláh

Each Day

256   O Lord, light up the small duties of this life.
May they shine with the beauty of your
countenance. May we believe that glory can
dwell in the commonest tasks of every day.

Saint Augustine

For Us All

257   We beseech Thee, Lord, to behold us with favor,
folk of many families and nations gathered
together in the peace of this roof, weak men and
women subsisting under the covert of Thy
patience.

Be patient still; suffer us yet awhile longer, with
our broken purposes of good, with our idle
endeavors against evil.

Suffer us awhile longer to endure, and (if it may
be) help us to do better.

Be with our friends, be with ourselves. Go with
each of us to rest; if any awake, temper to them
the dark hours of watching; and when the day
returns, return to us, our sun and comforter, and
call us up with morning faces and with morning
hearts—eager to labor—eager to be happy, if
happiness shall be our portion—and, if the day
be marked for sorrow, strong to endure it.

Robert Louis Stevenson

For the New Year

258   Exalted! Exalted! Exalted!
Ho, priestly people!
Let Bleku give peace.
Meat, meat,
Water, water,
Let blessings bless
Masses of food.

Ghanaian chant

259

*Lord, one day I will live with you
where you are. May you live with
me where I am now.*

John Mason Neale

Let God

260   I have become Thy servant, Thy slave.
Save me in the way that seems wise to Thee.

Tūkārâm

The God Who Answers

261   My God, last forever.
My God, grant me a girdle, multicolored,
    of sons and daughters.
My God, grant me to smell the fragrance
    of your life that shines forever.
My God, we are never full of your life.
My God, answer to what I told you.
And God said: "All right."

Samburu people of Kenya

262   *Teach us to pray often; that we*
may pray oftener.

Jeremy Taylor

God of Many

263   O God of many names—
Father, Mother, Spirit,
Compassionate One—
Look on us with mercy.

We close our eyes in prayer
And see your face
In our reflections,
Content with what we understand.

In our worship-places
Of stone and wood, sunshine and air,
Surrounded by organ, pipes, incense,
Smoke and drums—

Teach us to see beyond
The clouds of eye and skin and hair.
To treasure rivers and children
And creatures running free.

And to refrain from using you
As a excuse to harm any part
Of your creation.

Lynn Baquie

Make Me a Channel
of God's Peace

Golden Rules

✦

For the Grace to Work and Serve

✦

For Perseverance, Courage, and the
Completion of Good Undertakings

✦

Peace and Unity

Golden Rules

Every single creature is full of God and is a book about God. Every creature is a word about God. If I spent enough time with the tiniest creature—even a caterpillar—I would never have to prepare a sermon. So full of God is every creature.
—Meister Eckhart

He who is able to love himself is able to love others also; he who has learned to overcome self-contempt has overcome his contempt for others.
—Paul Tillich

Golden Rules

264   Give me such blessings as will lead to the good of others.

Devadas

The Way of Empathy

265   *Hinduism*

This is the sum of all righteousness: do nothing
to your neighbor which you would not have
him do to you after.

Zoroastrianism

That nature only is good when it shall not do to
another whatever is not good for its own self.

Jainism

A man of religion should treat all beings as he
himself would be treated.

Buddhism

Hurt not others in ways that you yourself would
find hurtful.

Confucianism

Surely it is a maxim of loving-kindness: do not
to others that which you would not have them
do to you.

Taoism

Regard your neighbor's gain as your own gain,
and your neighbor's loss as your own loss.

Judaism

What is hateful to you, do not do to your fellow
men. That is the entire Law; the rest is
commentary.

Christianity

Whatever you wish that men would do to you,
do so to them; for this is the law of the
prophets.

Islam

No one of you is a believer until he desires for
his brother that which he desires for himself.

Sikhism

As you deem yourself, so deem others. Then you
shall become a partner in heaven.

Bahá'í (Bahá'u'llá)

Wish not for others what you wish not for
yourselves; fear God and be not of the prideful.
You are all created out of water, and unto dust
shall you return.

For the Grace to Work and Serve

And Moses said to God, Who am I, that I should go to Pharaoh, and that I should bring the children of Israel out of Egypt? And God said to Moses, Go, and I will be with your mouth and teach you what you shall say.
—Exodus 3 and 4

When you first begin, you find only darkness and as it were a cloud of unknowing. You don't know what this means except that in your will you feel a simple, steadfast intention reaching out towards God.
—From The Cloud of Unknowing

It isn't necessary to go out to the slums to find poverty and a lack of love. There is someone who suffers in every family.
—Mother Teresa of Calcutta

The Servant Song

266   Here am I! Send me.

Isaiah 6:8

Make Me an Instrument of Your Peace

267   Lord, make me an instrument of your peace.
Where there is hatred, let me sow love,
Where there is injury, pardon
Where there is doubt, faith,
Where there is despair, hope,
Where there is darkness, light,
Where there is sadness, joy.

O Divine Master, grant that I may not so much
seek to be consoled as to console,
not so much to be understood as to understand,
not so much to be loved, as to love;
for it is in giving that we receive,
it is in pardoning that we are pardoned,
it is in dying that we awake to eternal life.

Saint Francis of Assisi

Prayer One

268   Lord and Master, teach me to surrender
           totally to thee,
       To let go and give myself completely,
       To abandon all petty self-centered concerns
       And dissolve my illusory sense of separateness
           in the great sea of your omnipresence,
       To ignite my life as a lamp
           to illumine the world
       With that ever-shining light
       And to serve you by serving one and all—
       And, by constantly remembering
           and following thy example,
       Let my life reflect thy wisdom
               all day long.

                   Lama Surya Das

Teaching

269   Lord, educate us for a higher life, and let that life
       be begun here. May we be always in the school,
       always disciples, and when we are out in the
       world may we be trying to put into practice
       what we have learned at Jesus's feet. What he
       tells us in darkness may we proclaim in the light,
       and what he whispers in our ear in the closets
       may we sound forth upon the house-tops.

                   Charles H. Spurgeon

Equip Us to Serve

270   By this merit
         may I become enlightened.
       Having become enlightened
         may I defeat all evils.
       Through the endless storm of birth, illness, old
       age and death,
         may I help all beings to cross the ocean of
         suffering.

                    Mahayana Buddhist dedication
                    prayer

Waking Up

271   Waking up this morning, I smile.
       Twenty-four brand new hours are before me.
       I vow to live fully in each moment
       and to look at all beings with eyes of
         compassion.

                    Thich Nhat Hanh

The Servant's Prayer

272 May no one who encounters me
ever have an insignificant contact.
May the mere fact of our meeting
contribute to the fulfillment of their wishes.

May I be a protector of the helpless,
a guide to those travelling the path,
a boat to those wishing to cross over,
or a bridge or a raft.

May I be a lamp for those in darkness,
a home for the homeless,
and a servant to the world.

From the Bodhicaryavatara of
Shantideva

I Saw

273 I slept and dreamt that life was joy
I woke and saw that life was service
I acted and behold! service was joy.

Rabindranath Tagore

A Nun's Prayer

274   Lord
Thou knowest better than I know myself that I
am growing older and will some day be old.
Keep me from the fatal habit of thinking I must
say something on every subject and on every
occasion. Release me from craving to straighten
out everybody's affairs. Make me thoughtful
but not moody; helpful but not bossy. With my
vast store of wisdom, it seems a pity not to use
it all, but Thou knowest Lord that I want a few
friends at the end.

Keep my mind free from the recital of endless
details; give me wings to get to the point. Seal
my lips on my aches and pains: They are
increasing, and love of rehearsing them is
becoming sweeter as the years go by. I dare not
ask for grace enough to enjoy the tales of others'
pains, but help me to endure them with patience.

I dare not ask for improved memory, but for a
growing humility and a lessening cocksureness
when my memory seems to clash with the
memories of others. Teach me the glorious
lesson that occasionally I may be mistaken.

Keep me reasonably sweet: I do not want to be
a saint—some of them are so hard to live
with—but a sour old person is one of the
crowning works of the devil. Give me that
ability to see good things in unexpected places,
and talents in unexpected people. And give me,
O Lord, the grace to tell them so.
Amen.

Seventeenth century

Pure Hands

275   Strengthen my hand, O my God, that it may
      take hold of Thy Book with such steadfastness
      that the hosts of the world shall have no power
      over it. Guard it, then, from meddling with
      whatsoever doth not belong unto it. Thou art
      verily the Almighty, the Most Powerful.

> Bahá'í prayer, daily while
> washing the hands

You Are Christ's Hands

276   Christ has no body now on earth but yours,
           no hands but yours,
           no feet but yours.
      Yours are the eyes through which is to look out
           Christ's compassion to the world;
      Yours are the feet with which he is to go about
           doing good;
      Yours are the hands with which he is to bless
           men now.

> Saint Teresa of Avila

Serve the Lord with Gladness

277   Make a joyful noise unto the Lord,
        all ye lands.
    Serve the Lord with gladness:
        come before his presence with singing.
    Know ye that the Lord he is God:
        it is he that hath made us,
    and not we ourselves;
    We are his people
        and the sheep of his pasture.

    Enter into his gates with thanksgiving,
        and into his courts with praise:
    Be thankful unto him,
        and bless his name.
    For the Lord is good;
        his mercy is everlasting;
    And his truth endureth
        to all generations.

                    Psalm 100

Mercy

278 Here is thy footstool and there rest thy feet
where live the poorest, and lowliest, and lost.
When I try to bow to thee, my obeisance
cannot reach down the depth where thy feet rest
among the poorest, and lowliest, and lost.
Pride can never approach to where thou walkest
in the clothes of the humble among the poorest,
and lowliest, and lost.
My heart can never find its way to where thou
keepest company with the companionless
among the poorest, the lowliest, and the lost.

Rabindranath Tagore

I Ask Only

279 Maker and High Priest,
I ask Thee not my joys to multiply,
Only to make me worthier of the least.

Elizabeth Barrett Browning

Perfect Humility

280   Do not give me riches, God,
that may make me proud;
nor poverty, that may deject me.

Give me, God, some help that I may serve you,
and life that I may praise you
and death that I may find salvation.

Marrano prayer

I Am Willing

281   Lord, I seek little of this
world's wealth.
If I may only be allowed to live and serve you, I
would be content.
If, however, this seems too much
in the eyes of those who persecute me,
I am willing to give up my life
before I forsake my faith.

Ferreolus of Vienne

Meaning

282   O Lord, let me not live to be useless; for Christ's
sake. Amen.

John Wesley

Work

283   God give me work
Till my life shall end
And life
Till my work is done.

Epitaph of Winifred Holtby

Walking by Faith

284   Walking by faith, let us do good works.

Saint Augustine

Self-Mastery

285   O Lord, help us to be masters of ourselves, that
we may be servants of others.

Sir Alexander Paterson

Beatitudes

286   Blessed are the poor in spirit
for theirs is the kingdom of heaven.
Blessed are those who mourn,
for they shall be comforted.
Blessed are the meek,
for they shall inherit the earth.
Blessed are those who hunger and thirst after
righteousness
for they shall be satisfied.
Blessed are the merciful,
for they shall obtain mercy.
Blessed are the pure in heart,
for they shall see God.
Blessed are the peacemakers,
for they shall be called children of God.
Blessed are those who are persecuted for
righteousness's sake,
for theirs is the kingdom of heaven.

Matthew 5:3-10

Speak, Lord, for Your Servant Is Listening

287   Speak, Lord, for your servant is listening.
Incline my heart to your words, and let your
speech come upon me as dew upon the grass.

In days gone by the children of Israel said to
Moses, "Speak to us and we shall listen; do not
let the Lord speak to us, lest we die."

This is not how I pray, Lord. No. With the
great prophet Samuel, I humbly and earnestly
beg: "Speak, Lord, for your servant is listening."

So, do not let Moses speak to me, but you, O
Lord, my God, eternal Truth, you speak to me.

If I hear your voice, may I not be condemned
    for hearing the word and not following it,
        for knowing it and not loving it,
            for believing it and not living it.

Speak then, Lord, for your servant listens, for
you have the words of eternal life. Speak to me
to comfort my soul and to change my whole
life; in turn, may it give you praise and glory
and honor, forever and ever.

Amen.

Thomas à Kempis

For the Asking

288   Give me, O Lord,
A steadfast heart, which no unworthy affection
may drag downwards;
Give me an unconquered heart, which no
tribulation can wear out;
Give me an upright heart, which no unworthy
purpose may tempt aside.
Impart to me also, O God,
understanding to know you,
diligence to seek you
a way of life to please you,
and a faithfulness that may embrace you.

Saint Thomas Aquinas

To Serve the Lord

289   Teach us, good Lord, to serve you as you
deserve; to give and not to count the cost; to
fight for you and not to heed the wounds; to
toil and not to seek for rest; to labor and not to
ask for any reward, except the knowledge that
we do your will.

Saint Ignatius of Loyola

For Perseverance, Courage, and the Completion of Good Undertakings

---

Our lives lose direction the moment they cease to be a voyage for the discovery of God.
—Author unknown

Strengthen My Soul

290   O God, who was and is,
      you willed that I should be born.
      You brought me to salvation
      through the waters of baptism.
      Be with me now and strengthen my soul
      that I will not weaken.
      Praise to God who has looked upon me
      and delivered me from my enemies.

Crispina of Thagara

Before the Armada

291   O Lord God, when Thou givest to Thy servants
to endeavor any great matter, grant us also to
know that it is not the beginning but the
continuing of the same until it be thoroughly
finished which yieldeth the true glory.

> Sir Francis Drake on the day of
> his raid against the Spanish fleet
> in Cádiz, 1587

The Prayer Warrior

292   O God our Father, let us not be content to wait
and see what will happen, but give us the
determination to make the right things happen.

While time is running out, save us from
patience which is akin to cowardice.

> Peter Marshall

Completion

293 Look upon us and hear us, O Lord our God;
and as you have given the first act of will, so
give the completion of the work; grant that we
may be able to finish what you have granted us
the wish to begin.

Mozarabic Liturgy

Sayings of the Fathers

294 Teach us, Lord, that it is not for us to complete
the work,
but neither may we desist from it:
    Do God's will as if it were your will, so that
    God
    may do your will as if it were God's will.

Jewish prayer and proverb

A Right-Sized Hope

295   Grant, O our God, that we may know you, love
you, and rejoice in you;
And if in this life we cannot do these things fully,
Grant that we may at least progress in them
from day to day, for Christ's sake. Amen.

Saint Anselm

Complete in Us

296   Give perfection to beginner, give intelligence to
the little ones, give aid to those who are running
their course. Give compunction to the
negligent, give fervor of spirit to the lukewarm,
give to the perfect a good consummation.

Gallican Sacramentary

For Fortitude

297   Here I stand, I can do no other. May God help
me! Amen.

Martin Luther, brought before the
Diet at Worms and saying "I cannot
and will not retract."

God Sustains

298 O God, who in your loving-kindness both
begins and finishes all good things, grant that as
we glory in the beginnings of your grace, so we
may rejoice in its completion.

Leonine Sacramentary

Into Your Hands

299 Into your hands, O Lord,
    I commend my spirit.
For the name of Jesus,
    and in defense of the Church,
    I am willing to die.

Thomas à Becket

Before Trafalgar

300 We trust in the great Disposer of all events, and
in the justice of our cause. I thank God for this
great opportunity of doing my duty.

Admiral Lord Nelson

301   *O Lord, this world is full of fear.*
Make my fear into a prayer
for the fearful.

Henri Nouwen

Remind Me Patiently

302   O Lord, Thou knowest how busy I must be this
day. If I forget Thee, do not Thou forget me. . . .

Sir Jacob Astley, on his knees before
the battle of Edgehill, 1642

303   *O Lord, Almighty God.*
Deliver us from all
* threatening need of war.*

Rite of the Swedish Church

Peace and Unity

Pray for your enemies, that they may be holy and that all may be well with them. And should you think this is not serving God, rest assured that more than all prayers, this is indeed the service of God.
—The Talmud

Perfect Unity

304 O God, let us be united; let us speak in
harmony; let our minds apprehend alike;
Common be our prayer, common the end of
our assembly;
Common be our resolution; common be our
deliberation.
Alike be our feelings; unified be our hearts;
Common be our intentions; perfect be our
unity.

From the Rig Veda

Let the Souls of Thy People Be Cool

305   Our Father, it is Thy universe,
       it is Thy will,
       let us be at peace,
       let the souls of Thy people be cool;
       Thou art our Father,
       remove all evil from our path.

                Prayer of the Nuer people of Africa

---

306   *O God, hear my voice, and grant*
       unto the world your
       everlasting peace.

                Pope John Paul II in Hiroshima

Diversity

307 In that which we share,
let us see the common prayer of humanity.
In that in which we differ,
let us wonder at the freedom of humankind.

Jewish prayer

Unite

308 O God!
Make good that which is between us,
unite our hearts
and guide us to paths of peace.

Muslim prayer

Sikh Prayer of The One

309   Some remember God as Ram;
          some call him Khuda;
       Some use the name Gosain;
          some worship him as Allah.
       Gracious Lord Almighty,
          you are the source and cause of everything,
       O Lord, Compassionate One,
          Shower your grace on all.
       Some bathe at Hindu holy places;
          some go to perform the Hajj;
       Some engage in Puja;
          some bow their heads in prayer;
       Some study Vedas;
          some read the Bible or Qur'an.
       Some dress in blue;
          some wear white;
       Some call themselves Muslims;
          some are called Hindus,
       Some desire to go to heaven;
          some long for paradise.
       But whoever does the will of God,
       To him all things are revealed.

                 Guru Arjan

Acceptance

310 O God we are one with you. . . .

Help us to realize that there can be no
understanding where there is mutual rejection.

O God, in accepting one another
wholeheartedly, fully, completely, we accept you,
and we thank you, and we adore you;
and we love you with our whole being,
    because our being is in your being,
    our spirit is rooted in your spirit.

Fill us then with love, and let us be bound
together with love as we go our diverse ways,
united in this one spirit which makes you
present to the world,
and which makes you witness to the ultimate
reality that is love.

Love has overcome.

Love is victorious.

Amen.

Thomas Merton

Thanksgiving Prayer

311   May the lamp of love
which eternally burns above
kindle divine fire
     in our hearts,
and fan that innate spark
of divinity
     into flame—
illumining all, opening our eyes
and consuming our differences,
driving the shadows
     from our faces.

As love dawns
on the horizon, may our community
awaken in the kingdom
of true communion,
which is at hand
     always.

May we learn to love
     one another
better even
than we love ourselves.

God is great—
may His grace be made manifest.

Love is stronger than death,
     Yes.

          Amen.

          Lama Surya Das

For Diverse Blessings

312　In mercy you have seen fit today to show me,
poor as I am,
how we can in no way pass judgment
on other people's intentions.
Indeed, by sending people along an endless
variety of paths,
you give me an example for myself,
and for this I thank you.

Saint Catherine of Siena

Prayer of the Midnight Service

313　O Lord and Master of my life,
give me not a spirit of sloth,
vain curiosity, lust for power and idle talk.

But give to me, your servant,
a spirit of soberness,
humility, patience and love.

Yea, O Lord and King,
grant me to see my own faults,
and not to condemn my brother;
for blessed are you to the ages of ages.
Amen.

Saint Ephraim the Syrian

And Peace

314   O God, from whom all holy desires, all good
      counsels and all just words do proceed, give unto
      us the same peace which the world cannot give.

                  Medieval English primer

Right Forgetting

315   O God of love, who gave us a commandment
      that we should love one another, even as you
      loved us and gave your beloved son for our life
      and salvation; we pray you to give us, your
      servants, in all times of our life on the earth, a
      mind forgetful of past ill-will, and a heart to
      love our brothers and sisters.

                  Coptic liturgy of Saint Cyril,
                  fifth century

316   *O God, help us not to despise or oppose
        what we do not understand.*

                William Penn

Gift of the Spirit

317   O merciful God, fill our hearts with the graces
        of your Holy Spirit—with love, joy, peace, long-
        suffering, gentleness, goodness, faith, meekness,
        temperance. Teach us to love those who hate
        us; to pray for those who despitefully use us;
        that we may be your children, our Father, who
        make your sun to shine on the evil and on the
        good and send rain on the just and on the
        unjust.

                Saint Anselm

Prayer for Peace

318   Supreme Lord,
       let there be peace in the sky and in the air,
       peace in the plant world and in the forests;
       let the cosmic powers be peaceful;
       let Brahma be peaceful;
       let there be undiluted and all-fulfilling peace
       everywhere.

                    The Atharva Veda

Mine Enemies

319   Almighty God have mercy on all that bear me
       evil will and would me harm; and their faults
       and mine together, by such easy, tender,
       merciful means, as your infinite wisdom best
       can devise, do please amend and redress, and
       make us saved souls in heaven together where
       we may even live and love together with you
       and your blessed Saints. . . .

                    Thomas More, imprisoned in
                    the Tower of London

Fierce Hope

320   Much remains
To conquer still; peace hath her victories
No less renowned than war; new foes arise,
Threatening to bind our souls with secular
    chains.
Help us to save free conscience from the paw
Of hireling wolves, whose gospel is their maw.

John Milton

The Way

321   The highest form of goodness is like water:
The goodness of water benefits all peoples
And does not strive:
Water is content with places detested by men.
So is the Way.

Tao-te-Ching

Peace Seeds:
Twelve Prayers for Peace Prayed in Assisi, Italy

322   *A Hindu Prayer for Peace*

O God, lead us from the unreal to the Real. O
God lead us from darkness to light. O God,
lead us from death to immortality. Shanti,
Shanti, Shanti unto all. O Lord God almighty,
may there be peace in celestial regions. May
there be peace on earth. May the waters be
appeasing. May herbs be wholesome, and may
trees and plants bring peace to all. May all
beneficent beings bring peace to us. May your
Vedic Law propagate peace all through the
world. May all things be a source of peace to us.
And may your peace itself bestow peace on all,
and may that peace come to me also.

A Buddhist Prayer for Peace

May all beings everywhere plagued with
sufferings of body and mind quickly be freed
from their illnesses. May those frightened cease
to be afraid, and may those bound be free. May
the powerless find power, and may people think
of befriending one another. May those who find
themselves in trackless, fearful wildernesses—the
children, the aged, the unprotected—be guarded
by beneficent celestials, and may they swiftly
attain Buddhahood.

A Jainist Prayer for Peace

Peace and Universal Love is the essence of the Gospel preached by all the Enlightened Ones. The Lord has preached that equanimity is the Dharma. Forgive do I creatures all, and let all creatures forgive me. Unto all have I amity, and unto none enmity. Know that violence is the root of all miseries in the world. Violence is the knot of bondage. "Do not injure any living being." This is the eternal, perennial, and unalterable way of spiritual life. A weapon, howsoever powerful it may be, can always be superseded by a superior one; but no weapon can be superior to nonviolence and love.

A Muslim Prayer for Peace

In the name of Allah, the beneficent, the merciful. Praise be to the Lord of the Universe who has created us and made us into tribes and nations, that we may know each other, not that we may despise each other.
If the enemy incline towards peace, do thou also incline towards peace, and trust in God, for the Lord is the one that heareth and knoweth all things. And the servants of God, Most Gracious are those who walk on the earth in humility, and when we address them, we say, "Peace."

A Sikh Prayer for Peace

"God adjudges us according to our deeds, not
the coat that we wear." That Truth is above
everything, but higher still is truthful living.
Know that we attain God when we love, and
only that victory endures in consequence of
which no one is defeated.

A Bahá'í Prayer for Peace

Be generous in prosperity, and thankful in
adversity. Be fair in your judgment, and
guarded in your speech. Be a lamp unto those
who walk in darkness, and a home to the
stranger. Be eyes to the blind, and a guiding
light unto the feet of the erring. Be a breath of
life to the body of humankind, a dew to the soil
of the human heart, and a fruit upon the tree of
humility.

A Shinto Prayer for Peace

Although the people living across the ocean
surrounding us, I believe, are all our brothers
and sisters—why are there constant troubles in
this world? Why do winds and waves rise in
the ocean surrounding us?
I only earnestly wish that the wind will soon
puff away all the clouds which are hanging over
the tops of the mountains.

An African Prayer for Peace

Almighty God, the Great Thumb we cannot evade to tie any knot; the roaring Thunder that splits mighty trees: the all-seeing Lord up on high who sees even the footprints of antelope on a rock mass here on Earth. You are the one who does not hesitate to respond to our call. You are the cornerstone of peace.

A Native American Prayer for Peace

O Great Spirit of our Ancestors, I raise my pipe to you. To your messengers the four winds, and to Mother Earth who provides for your children: Give us the wisdom to teach our children to love, to respect and to be kind to each other so that they may grow with peace in mind. Let us learn to share all the good things that you provide for us on this Earth.

A Zoroastrian Prayer for Peace

We pray to God to eradicate all the misery in the world: that understanding triumph over ignorance, that generosity triumph over indifference, that trust triumph over contempt, and that truth triumph over falsehood.

A Jewish Prayer for Peace

Come let us go up to the mountain of the Lord, that we may walk the paths of the Most High. And we shall beat our swords into plowshares, and our spears into pruning hooks. Nation shall not lift up sword against nation—neither shall they learn war anymore. And none shall be afraid, for the mouth of the Lord of Hosts has spoken.

A Christian Prayer for Peace

Blessed are the peacemakers, for they shall be known as the Children of God. But I say to you that hear, love your enemies, do good to those who hate you, bless those who curse you, pray for those who abuse you. To those who strike you on the cheek, offer the other also, and from those who take away your cloak, do not withhold your coat as well. Give to everyone who begs from you and of those who take away your goods, do not ask them again. And as you wish that others would do to you, do so to them.

> Prayed on the United Nations Day
> of Prayer for World Peace, 1986

Shanti! Shanti! Shanti!

323 May there be peace in heaven,
  may there be peace in the skies,
May there be peace on earth,
  may there be peace in the waters,
May there be peace in the plants,
  may there be peace in the trees,
May we find peace in all the diving powers,
  may we find peace in the supreme Lord,
May we all be in peace,
  may that peace be mine.

Peace! Peace! Peace!

The Vedas

A City of God

324 O God, grant us a vision of this city, fair as it might be: a city of justice, where none shall prey upon the other; a city of plenty, where vice and poverty shall cease to fester; a city of brotherhood, where success is founded on service, and honor is given to nobleness alone; a city of peace where order shall not rest on force, but on the love of all for each and all.

Walter Rauschenbusch

America

325   Our fathers' God! to Thee,
Author of Liberty,
To Thee we sing:
Long may our land be bright
With freedom's holy light;
Protect us by Thy might,
Great God, our King!

Samuel Francis Smith

With Malice Toward None

326   Grant, O merciful God, that with malice toward
none, with charity for all, with firmness in the
right as you give us to see the right, we may
strive to finish the work we are in; to bind up
the nation's wounds; to care for him who shall
have borne the battle and for his widow and his
orphan; to do all which may achieve and cherish
a just and lasting peace among ourselves and
with all nations.

Abraham Lincoln

Shelter Prayer

327 Increase, O God the spirit of neighborliness
     among us, that in peril we may uphold one
     another, in calamity serve one another, in
     suffering tend one another, and in homelessness,
     loneliness of exile befriend one another. Grant
     us brave and enduring hearts that we may
     strengthen one another, till the disciplines and
     testing of these days be ended, and Thou dost
     give again peace in our time.

                    Used in English air-raid shelters
                    during World War II

328 *O Lord, baptize our hearts into a*
     sense of the conditions and needs
     of all people.

                    George Fox

Nkosi Sikilel i Afrika

329　Have compassion, Lord
　　　upon this land.
　　　Let your mercy
　　　come upon it
　　　Lord.
　　　Hold your hands out
　　　Lord
　　　and bless this land
　　　land that burns
　　　Lord
　　　land that burns.
　　　Let our people stand
　　　before you
　　　all.
　　　Judge them with
　　　your judgment
　　　hard, O Lord.
　　　Let justice triumph
　　　in this land
　　　land that burns
　　　Lord
　　　land that burns.

South African national anthem

Both

330   O God,
to those who have hunger
give bread;
And to us who have bread
give the hunger for justice.

Latin American prayer

O Great Spirit

331   O Great Spirit, Creator and source of every
blessing, we pray that you will bring peace to all
our brothers and sisters of this world. Give us
wisdom to teach our children to love, to respect
and to be kind to each other. Help us to learn
to share all the good things that you provide for
us. Bless all who share this meal with us today.
We ask your special blessing on those who are
hungry today, especially little children. Help us
to be just and to bring your peace to all the
earth. Praise and Thanksgiving be to you.
Amen.

Author unknown

Deep Peace

332 Deep peace
         of the running wave to you,
     Deep peace
         of the quiet earth to you,
     Deep peace
         of the flowing air to you,
     Deep peace
         of the shining star to you.

Gaelic blessing

Prayers for Protection

Prayers in Times of Trial

Prayers in Times of Trial

We do not know how we ought to pray, but the Spirit himself pleads with God for us.
—Saint Paul, Romans 8:26

Our Vessel

333 Frail is our vessel, and the ocean is wide; but as in your mercy you have set our course, so steer the vessel of our life towards the everlasting shore of peace, and bring us at length to the quiet haven of our heart's desire, where you, O God, are blessed, and live and reign for ever and ever.

Saint Augustine

A Prayer for the Sixth Hour of the Day

334   O Lord,
       you who have measured
       the heights and the earth
       in the hollow of your hand,
       and created the six-wing Seraphim
       to cry out to you with an unceasing voice
       Holy, Holy, Holy:
       Glory to your name!

       Deliver me
       from the mouth of the evil one, O Master.
       Forget my many evil deeds
       and through the multitude of your compassions
       grant me daily forgiveness,
       for you are blessed unto the ages.

              Saint Sarrah

---

335   *Lord, I am oppressed:*
       Undertake for me.

              Hezekiah, King of Judah
              (Isaiah 38:14)

A Shield

336   Cause us, our Father, to lie down in peace, and
rise again to enjoy life. Spread over us the
covering of your peace, guide us with your good
counsel and save us for the sake of your name.
Be a shield about us, turning away every enemy,
disease, violence, hunger and sorrow.

Shelter us in the shadow of your wings, for you
are a God who guards and protects us, a ruler of
mercy and compassion. Guard us when we go
out and when we come in, to enjoy life and
peace both now and forever, and spread over us
the shelter of your peace.

From the Jewish daily service

Who Delivers Us From Evil

337   Whosoever propitiates the immortal, bright,
swift-horsed Sun, he also propitiates Mihr, the
forest-dweller of a thousand ears, of ten
thousand eyes.

He propitiates the forest-dweller Mihr's mace,
which is well directed at the skulls of demons.

I propitiate the One who is better than all
friends.

Zoroastrian litany to the Sun

Charm for Fear by Night

338   God before me, God behind me,
God above me, God below me;
I on the path of God,
God upon my track.

Who is there on land?
Who is there on wave?
Who is there on billow?
Who is there by door-post?
Who is along with us?
God and Lord.

I am here abroad,
I am here in need,
I am here in pain,
I am here in straits,
I am here alone.
O God, aid me.

from the *Carmina Gadelica*

Out of the Deep

339   Out of the deep I have called to you, O Lord:
Lord, hear my voice.

Psalm 130:1

The Sea Is So Wide

340   Dear God, be good to me. The sea is so wide,
       and my boat is so small.

                    Breton fisherman's prayer

Seafarer's Prayer

341   Heavenly Father:
       We pray to you for those on the perilous ocean,
       that you will embrace them with your mighty
       protection
       and grant them success in all their rightful
       undertakings.

       Grant them in all hours of need to perceive that
       they have a God who remembers them,
       and grant them grace in the hour of danger to
       commit their souls into your hands.

       O Lord Jesus Christ, who can rebuke the storm
       and bring it to silence, and lay the roaring waves
       to rest,
       show them who call to you out of the deep
       that you hear their prayer
       and will save them.

       And finally, bring us all to the only safe port.

                    Fom the ancient Swedish rite

Navy Hymn

342   Eternal Father! Strong to save,
Whose arm hath bound the restless wave,
Who bidd'st the mighty ocean deep
Its own appointed limits keep;
   Oh, hear us when we cry to Thee
   For those in peril on the sea!

William Whiting

343

*Over the immense store of sea-
water ships sail, but how can my
little broken checkerboard raft cross
to the opposite shore?*

Mahīpati

Hazard

344   Grandfather, Great Father, let matters go well
with me, for I am going into the forest.

Bambuti Pygmy prayer

The Lord Is My Shepherd

345   The Lord is my shepherd; I shall not want.
He makes me to lie down in green pastures:
he leads me beside the still waters.
He restores my soul: he leads me in the paths of
righteousness for his name's sake.
Yea, though I walk through the valley of the
shadow of death, I will fear no evil: for you are
with me; your rod and your staff they
comfort me.
You prepare a table before me in the presence of
my enemies: you anoint my head with oil; my
cup runs over.
Surely goodness and mercy shall follow me all
the days of my life: and I will dwell in the house
of the Lord for ever.

Psalm 23

---

346   *The eternal God is our dwelling*
place, and underneath are
the everlasting arms.

Deuteronomy 33:27

Extremis

347   *Run to my help, Dear Ram. To what extremity
are you willing to see me suffer?*

Death is attacking me. How is it that
    compassion does not arise in you?
I shall look on you to my heart's content.
And I shall wipe your feet with the hair of
    my head;
My eyes are weary, waiting for you, dear Lord,
When will you come?

In my millions and millions of rebirths my heart
    is ever on fire.
O Ram, pour down on me the flood of you
    compassion.
Give peace to my troubled heart, O Ram,
Ocean-of-Mercy.
Destroy my connection with the six enemies of
    the soul.[1]

What does an infant know of the love of its
    mother and father?
What can a calf know of its mother's love, when
    driven away before tasting its mother's milk?
Fishes, though living in the water, do not know
    the water.
So though continually beside you, I have missed
    seeing you, O Mass-of-Goodness.

---

1. The six enemies of the soul are Lust, Anger,
Covetousness, Inordinate Affection, Pride, and Envy.

Many of your servants gave themselves to
    austerities, or wandered to sacred places.
Some lived in the caves of the mountains, where
    they met no human being.
Listening to their mode of life I am overcome
    with great wonder.
But I, your servant, have lived a life of no value.

How great a burden shall I impose on Ram?
Will He not get wearied with me?
Yet the Protector-of-the-Lowly will run to my
    help when in distress.
And through Him this body of mine will
    have peace.

What a Ram I have, Giver of salvation!
Through Him all my concern has vanished.
What can I render to Him, Almighty One,
    in return?
I must at least praise Him with my lips for ever
    and ever.

                    Ramdas

---

348   *Though the heavens boom with*
        thunder, though the sphere of the
        universe crack into pieces, though
        fire devour the three worlds, yet
        will I wait on you, O Lord.

                    Eknath

Prayer of Joyful Assurance

349   Our Father, who art in Heaven!
I am in thy kingdom.
May thy name
Be kept holy!

May thy Spirit come, O King
And give life to thy people!

> Hymn and chorus,
> Zulu Nazarite church

---

350   *Death came to sting me. But he*
changed into a Merciful one. Now
I know him well. For heart has
met heart.

> Eknath

The Lord's Prayer

351 Our Father, who art in heaven,
     hallowed be thy name.
     Thy kingdom come;
     thy will be done on earth as it is in heaven.
     Give us this day our daily bread;
     and forgive us our trespasses
     as we forgive those who trespass against us;
     and lead us not into temptation,
     but deliver us from evil.

Matthew 6:9-13

For thine is the kingdom
and the power, and the glory
forever and ever. Amen.

Ancient liturgical ending,
ca. 100 A.D.

A Prayer from Prison

352 The hour for my departure is at hand.
     I have fought a good fight,
     I have finished the course,
     I have kept the faith.
Now, the prize awaits me,
     the crown of righteousness,
Which the Lord, the righteous judge,
     will award me on that day;
And not me only, but all who love his appearing.
The Lord will deliver me
     from all evil,
     and take me safely into his heavenly kingdom.
To him be glory forever
     and ever! Amen.

Saint Paul, in 2 Timothy 4:6–8, 4:18

And May He Come

353 And may he come to us for help,
     And may he come to us for freedom,
     And may he come to us for joy,
     And may he come to us for mercy,
     And may he come to us for healing,
     And may he come to us for victory,
     And may he come to us for well-being,
     And may he come to us and sanctify us:
He, the mighty one, the all-powerful.
The undeceived one.
The Lord of wide pastures.

The Avesta

Asking God

354   God, be propitious to me!
Here is the New Moon:
Keep every harmful sickness far from me.
Stop the wicked man who is contemplating my
misfortune:
Let his wicked plans fall on himself.
O God, be propitious to me!
Desert me not in my need:
Give me wives, children, slaves and wealth.
Lead to my house guests of happiness, O God!

Duala prayer of Cameroon

That I Might Love My Enemy

355   Grant me prudently to avoid the one who
flatters me, and patiently to bear with the one
who contradicts me; for it is a mark of wisdom
not to give ear to the wicked flattery of the
siren, nor to be moved by every wind of words.

Thomas à Kempis

The Breastplate

356 I bind unto myself today
The power of God to hold and lead,
His eye to watch, his might to stay,
His ear to hearken to my need.
The wisdom of my God to teach,
His hand to guide, his shield to ward;
The word of God to give me speech,
His heavenly host to be my guard.

Christ be with me, Christ within me,
Christ behind me, Christ before me,
Christ beside me, Christ to win me,
Christ to comfort and restore me,
Christ beneath me, Christ above me,
Christ in quiet, Christ in danger,
Christ in mouth of friend or stranger.

I bind unto myself the name,
The strong name of the Trinity;
By invocation of the same,
The Three in One, the One in Three,
Of whom all nature hath creation;
Eternal Father, Spirit, Word,
Praise to the Lord of my salvation,
Salvation is of Christ the Lord.

Saint Patrick of Ireland

Hope

357   And now unto him who is able to keep us from
falling and lift us from the dark valley of despair
to the bright mountain of hope, from the
midnight of desperation to the daybreak of joy;
to him be power and authority, for ever and ever.

Martin Luther King, Jr.

Grace and Thanksgiving

One of the best ways to worship God
is simply to be happy.
—Traditional Hindu wisdom

Grace

358   Thank you very, very much;
my God, thank you.
Give me food today,
food for my sustenance every day.
Thank you very, very much.

Samburu prayer, Kenya

Bless This Food

359   O Lord of the universe
       Please accept all this food
       It was given by you
       Let it be of service to all
       Only you can bless it.

Bhagavad Gita

Contemplation of the Bodhisattva Buddhists

360   This food comes from the Earth and the Sky,
       It is the gift of the entire universe
       And the fruit of much hard work:
       May we live in a way that makes us worthy
          to receive it.

Traditional

Jewish Blessing

361   Blessed are you
       O Lord our God
       king of the world
       who brings forth bread from the earth.

Traditional

Muslim Grace

362   In the name of Allah!
    (before eating)
Bi Ismillaahi!

Thanks to Allah, Master of both worlds!
    —this and the afterworld
    (after eating)
Al Hamdu Lillaahi Rabbil 'Aalamin!

Traditional

Homage

363   Salutations!
O Merciful God who provides food for the body
and soul, you have kindly granted what is spread
before us. We thank you.
Bless the loving hands that prepared this meal
and
us who are to enjoy it, please.
Homage, homage,
homage to thee!

Tamil prayer

Fasting

364 We beseech you, O Lord, let your gracious favor
carry us through the fast which we have begun;
that as we observe it by bodily discipline, so we
may be able to fulfil it with sincerity of mind.

Gelasian Sacramentary

For Bread and Wine

365 Eternal spirit of Justice and Love,
At this time of thanksgiving we would be aware
of our dependence on the earth and on the
sustaining presence of other human beings
both living and gone before us.
As we partake of bread and wine, may we
remember that there are many for whom
sufficient bread is a luxury, or for whom
wine, when attainable, is only an escape.
Let our thanksgiving for Life's bounty include a
commitment to changing the world, that
those who are now hungry may be filled and
those without hope may be given courage.
Amen.

Congregation of Abraxas

One Thing More

366   To all else you have given us,
      O Lord,
      we ask for but one thing more:
      Give us
      grateful hearts.

George Herbert

Scottish Blessing for Food

367   Some hae meat and canna eat,
      And some wad eat that want it;
      But we hae meat, and we can eat,
      And sae the Lord be thankit.

Robert Burns

Before Meals

368   This ritual is one
      This food is one
      We who offer the food are one
      The fire of hunger is also one
      All action is one
      We who understand this are one.

Ancient Hindu blessing

For the Fires of Our Cooking Pots

369   O Great Spirit, now that I am about to eat,
      give my thanks to the beast and birds
      whom You have provided for my hunger,
      and pray deliver my sorrow
      that living things must make a sacrifice
      for my comfort and well-being.
      Let the feather of corn spring up in its time
      and let it not wither but make full grains
      for the fires of our cooking pots,
      now that I am about to eat.

                    Native American prayer

For All God's Gifts

370   The ungrateful man overlooks ten gifts from God,
      But when one is withheld, loses his faith.
      If God were to withdraw the other ten as well,
      What could he do?

      We cannot force God's hand;
      Better that we should submit to his will.
      He who delights in the will of God,
      Happiness will be his.
      Whomever God inspires to follow his way
      Gains every possible blessing.

                    Guru Arjan

Ancient Persian Grace

371   The Fire of Ahura Mazda
     gives command to all
     for whom he cooks
     the evening and the morning meal.

          Zoroastrian litany to the Fire

From the Sūryaśataka

372   Sūrya, the Hot-rayed, upon seeing mortals
     without covering at dawn—when darkness,
     whose guise is that of an upper garment, is
     slipping away—
   Spreads wide his rays, like the threads stretched
     by a weaver.
   And these rays, becoming dense, reveal at once
     the spotless sky
   Just as the threads, on being close-woven,
     fashion a spotless garment.
   May these rays of the Hot-rayed Sūrya bestow
     upon you abundance,
     and prosperity!

          Mayūra

Life Here and Hereafter

Walking in the Valley
of the Shadow of Death

Walking in the Valley
of the Shadow of Death

*Deep in the sea are riches beyond compare
But if you seek safety, it is on the shore.*
—Sheikh Saadi

*In the rush and noise of life, as you have intervals, step
within yourselves and be still. Wait upon God and feel
his good presence; this will carry you through your day's
business.*
—William Penn

Returning

373 Clear sky   *Sora saete*
      the way I came by once   *moto kishi michi o*
      I now go back by.   *kaeru nari*

          Gitoku, Japanese poet,
          on his death

Teach Us to Number Our Days

374   Lord, you have been our dwelling place through
      all generations.
Before the mountains were brought forth,
Or you had formed the earth and world,
From everlasting to everlasting you are God.
You bid us become, again, what we once were;
You turn us back into dust.
For a thousand years in your sight
Are like yesterday when it is past,
Or like a watch in the night.
You carry men away as with a flood; they are
      like a sleep.
In the morning they are like the new grass of
      the morning:
In the forenoon it flourishes, and grows up,
By evening it is cut down, and withers.
So teach us to number our days,
That we may apply our hearts to wisdom.

Psalm 90:1–6, 12

Time

375   In the time when God created all things,
God created the sun;
and the sun is born and dies and comes again.
God created the moon;
and the moon is born and dies and comes again.
God created the stars;
and the stars are born and die and come again.
God created humankind;
and a human being is born and dies . . .
and does not come again.

Dinka prayer, Sudan

Song of Simeon

376   Lord, now lettest thy servant depart in peace.

Luke 2:29

Receive Me, at My Death

377 Almighty and most merciful Father, I am now,
as to human eyes it seems, about to
commemorate, for the last time, the death of
your Son Jesus Christ our Savior and Redeemer.
Grant, O Lord, that my whole hope and
confidence may be in his merits and his mercy;
enforce and accept my imperfect repentance;
make this commemoration confirm my faith,
establish my hope and enlarge my charity, and
make the death of your Son Jesus Christ
effectual to my redemption. Have mercy upon
me and pardon the multitude of my offenses.
Bless my friends, have mercy upon all. Support
me, by the grace of your Holy Spirit, in the days
of weakness and at the hour of death; and
receive me, at my death, to everlasting
happiness, for the sake of Jesus Christ. Amen.

Samuel Johnson

I Have Held Out My Hands

378 I have held out my hands to you [in prayer],
And he who holds out his hands dies not.

Prayer from Angola

Into Your Hands

379   Grant me, merciful Savior, that when death has
shut up the eyes of my body, yet that the eye of
my soul may still behold and look upon you;
that when death has taken away the use of my
tongue and speech, yet that my heart may cry
and say unto you, *In manus tuas, Domine,
commendo spiritum meum:* that is to say, O
Lord, into thy hands I give and commit my
soul.

English Primer of 1559

A Branch of the Tree

380   This death, which seems so terrible,
is little enough to gain eternal life.
Savior, receive a branch of the tree;
it will decay, but will flower again
and be clothed in glory.
The vine dies in winter, yet revives in spring.
Shall not this life which is cut down rise again?
My hearth rejoices in the Lord,
and my soul has exulted in your salvation.

James Intercisus

Face to Face

381   Day after day, O lord of my life, shall I stand
before Thee face to face? With folded hands, O
lord of all world, shall I stand before Thee face
to face?
Under Thy great sky in solitude and silence,
with humble heart shall I stand before Thee face
to face?
In this laborious world of thing, tumultuous
with toil and with struggle, among hurrying
crowds shall I stand before Thee face to face?
And when my work shall be done in this world,
O King of kings, alone and speechless shall I
stand before Thee face to face?

Rabindranath Tagore

No Thing Greater

382   I enjoy life;
but love of life has not
made me afraid to die.
There is nothing greater than life—
that eternal life which gives
immortality to the soul of the righteous.

Attributed to Apollonius the
Apologist

Paradise

383   O gioia! O ineffabile allegrezza!
O vita intera d'amore e de pace!
O senza brama sicura ricchezza!

The Divine Comedy
of Dante Alighieri

O God, Our Help in Ages Past

384   Time, like an ever-rolling stream,
Bears all its sons away;
They fly, forgotten, as a dream
Dies at the opening day.

O God, our help in ages past,
Our hope for years to come,
Be Thou our guide while life shall last,
And our eternal home.

Isaac Watts

Prayer for the Church

385   Good God, may we confess your name
to the end;
May we emerge unmarked and glorious
from the traps and darkness of this world.
As you have bound us together
by charity and peace,
And as together we have persevered
under persecution,
So may we also rejoice together
in your heavenly kingdom.

Cyprian of Carthage

Prayer by Darkness

386   Be present, O merciful God, and protect us
through the silent hours of this night, so that we
who are fatigued by the changes and chances of
this fleeting world, may repose upon your
eternal changelessness.

Leonine Sacramentary

Our End

387   O Lord, you have made us very small, and we
bring our years to an end, like a tale that is told.
Help us to remember that beyond our brief day
is the eternity of your love.

Reinhold Niebuhr

You Know All About Me

388   O God, it was you who called me

and sent me to this place.
You know all about me—
the days I have lived
and the days that are left to me.
If it is your will to call me home,
I leave the decision to you.

Yona Kanamuzeyi

The Beginning

389   This is the end,
but for me
It is the beginning
of life.

Dietrich Bonhoeffer

You Have Prepared a Place for My Soul

390 O God, you have prepared a place for my soul,
prepare my soul for that place; prepare it with
holiness; prepare it with desire; and even while
it remains on earth, let it dwell in heaven with
you; seeing the beauty of your face and the
glory of your saints, now and for evermore.

Joseph Hall, Bishop of Norwich

Farewell

391 Returning thanks   *Shōgai no*
for life, I turn back and bow   *oreigaeshi ya*
eastward.   *higashi muki*

Goshi

Reunion

392 O God, my Master, should I gain the grace
To see you face to face when life is ended,
Grant that a little dog, who once pretended
That I was God, may see me face to face.

Francis Jammes

Heaven

393   The road I take   *Yuku michi wa*
      to paradise is bright   *hana ni akaruki*
      with flowers.   *jōdo kana*

      Sokin

Peace at the Last

394   O Lord, support us all the day long, until the
      shadows lengthen and the evening comes, and
      the busy world hushed, and the fever of life is
      over, and our work is done. Then in your
      mercy grant us a safe lodging, and a holy rest,
      and peace at the last.

      John Henry Newman

The Peace
That Passes
All Understanding

Blessings and Benedictions

Blessings and Benedictions

Finally, brethren, whatever things are true, whatever things are honest, whatever things are just, whatever things are pure, whatever things are lovely, whatever things are of good report; if there be any virtue, and if there be any praise, think on these things.
—Saint Paul's letter to the Philippians (4:8-9)

Blessing

395   The peace of God which passes all understanding, keep our hearts and minds in the knowledge and love of God, and of His Son Jesus Christ our Lord, and the blessing of God Almighty, the Father, the Son, and the Holy Spirit, be among you and remain with you always.

The Book of Common Prayer

May the Blessing of God Rest Upon You . . .

396 May his peace abide with you.
May his presence illuminate your heart
Now and forevermore.

Sufi blessing

Today, Tonight and Tomorrow

397 Bless to me, O God, the earth beneath my feet,
Bless to me, O God, the path whereon I go,
Bless to me, O God, the people whom I meet,
Today, tonight and tomorrow.

Celtic blessing

May God Hold You

398 May the road rise to meet you,
may the wind be always at your back,
may the sun shine warm on your face,
the rain fall softly on your fields;
and until we meet again,
may God hold you in the palm of his hand.

Gaelic blessing

Good Wishes

399   The good of eye be thine,
The good of liking be thine,
     The good of my heart's desire.

The good of sons be thine,
The good of daughters be thine,
     The good of the sap of my sense.

The good of sea be thine,
The good of land be thine,
     The good of the Prince of heaven.

✦

Each day be glad to thee,
No day be sad to thee,
     Life rich and satisfying.

Plenty be on thy course,
A son be on thy coming,
     A daughter on thine arriving.

The strong help of the serpent be thine,
The strong help of fire be thine,
     The strong help of the graces.

The love-death of joy be thine,
The love-death of Mary be thine,
     The loving arm of thy Savior.

From the *Carmina Gadelica*

For Blessing

400   Bless all who worship you,
from the rising of the sun
until the going down of the same.

Of your goodness, give us.
With your love, inspire us.
By your spirit, guide us.
By your power, protect us.
In your mercy, receive us now and always.

Ancient collect

Dismissal

401   Now unto him that is able to keep you from
falling, and to present you faultless before the
presence of his glory with exceeding joy,
To the only wise God our Savior, be glory and
majesty, dominion and power, both now and ever.
Amen.

Jude 24–25

The Lord Bless You and Keep You . . .

402   The Lord make his face to shine upon you,
and be gracious unto you:
The Lord lift up his countenance upon you,
and give you peace.

Numbers 6:24–26

Saints and Angels

403   Be each saint in heaven,
Each sainted woman in heaven,
Each angel in heaven
Stretching their arms for you,
Smoothing the way for you,
When you go thither
   Over the river hard to see;
Oh when you go thither home
   Over the river hard to see.

From the *Carmina Gadelica*

All Shall Be Well

404 But all shall be well
   and all shall be well,
      and all manner of things shall be well.

Julian of Norwich

---

405 *May you meet with the*
   Kindly-Disposed One!

African blessing

The Jewish Temple Blessing

406 The Lord bless us and keep us, the Lord make
   his face to shine upon us, and be gracious unto
   us, the Lord lift up his countenance upon us
   and give us peace, now and evermore.
   Amen.

Seventh century B.C.
(Numbers 6:24-26)

Doxology

407   Now to him who is able to do immeasurably more than all we ask or imagine, according to his power that is at work within us, to him be glory throughout all generations, for ever and ever.

Saint Paul, Ephesians 3:20–21

---

408   *May God's blessing be yours,*
And well may it befall you.

From the Carmina Gadelica

Rain

409   Like a vast cloud rising above the world
covering all things
everywhere—
a gracious cloud full of waters;
lightning erupts and dazzles,
thunder rumbles distantly,
bringing joy and relief to us all.

The dry ground is soaked,
herbs and trees flourish together.
From the one water which issued from that
cloud,
plants, trees, thickets, forests,
according to their need,
receive moisture.

In like manner the Buddha appears in the world
for the sake of the living:
   "I come to pour enrichment on all parched
   living beings,
   to free them from their misery.
   Everywhere impartially, forever to all beings,
   I preach the Law equally.
   Equally I rain the Law—rain untiringly."

    The Lotus Sutra

Dnyanadev's Benediction

410   And now may God, the Soul of the Universe,
Be pleased with this, my offering of words.
And being pleased, may He give me
This favor in return:

That the crookedness of evil men and women
    cease,
And the love of goodness grow in them.
May all beings experience from one another
The friendship of the heart.
May the darkness of sin disappear.
May the Universe see the rising of the Sun of
Righteousness.
Whatever is desired, may it be received
By every living being.

May the multitude of those who love God
And shower on humankind all forms of blessings;
May they constantly, on this earth,
Come in touch with its living beings.

May this forest of walking Wish-trees,
May this city built of living Wish-gems,
May this talking sea of nectar,
May these moons without dark spots,
May these suns without fierce heat,
May all these ever-good ones
Be the close kin of humankind.

And now in every form of happiness
May there be enjoyment to the full everywhere.
And may the Supreme Being be worshipped
For ever and ever.

Prayer of a Hindu poet-saint

Acknowledgments

Grateful acknowledgment is made to the following for permission to reprint material copyrighted or controlled by them. An exhaustive effort has been made to trace and locate rights holders and to clear reprint permissions. If any required acknowledgments have been omitted or any rights overlooked, it is unintentional. If notified, the publishers will be pleased to correct any omission in future editions. Names of prayers refer to titles used by the editor for this collection. This section constitutes a continuation of the copyright page.

Congregation of Abraxas for excerpts from *The Book of Hours*, © 1985. Reprinted by permission of the Congregation of Abraxas, A Unitarian Universalist Order for Liturgical and Spiritual Renewal.

For "Child's Prayer of Thanks," reprinted from *Mealtime Prayers* by Mildred Tengbom, copyright © 1985 Augsburg Publishing House. Used by permission of Augsburg Fortress.

Prayers by Lama Surya Das © Lama Surya Das, all rights reserved. Reprinted by permission of the author.

Horton Davies for a translation of "All in All" by François Fénelon. Used by permission.

Excerpt "Just to Be" from *The Insecurity of Freedom* by Abraham Joshua Heschel. Copyright © 1966 by Abraham Joshua Heschel. Copyright renewed © 1994 by Sylvia Heschel. Reprinted by permission of Farrar, Straus & Giroux, Inc.

Hancock House Publishers Ltd. for "Creation" by Chief Dan George ("And My Heart Soars"), from *Saanichtoni*, 1974. Used by permission of the publisher.

For "Prayers for Young People" excerpted from *The End of Religion: Autobiographical Explorations* by Dom Aelred Graham. Copyright © 1971 by Aelred Graham. Reprinted by permission of Harcourt Brace & Company.

Jacquetta Hawkes for version of Pharaoh Akhenaton's "Hymn to the Sun," from *Man in the Sun* by Jacquetta Hawkes, Random House, Inc. 1962. Reprinted by permission of Peters Fraser & Dunlop Group Ltd..

Holy Cross Orthodox Press for "Prayer of the Midnight Service," "A Prayer of the Sixth Hour of the Day," and "Recovery" (excerpts from "A Prayer to the Almighty God and Father...") from *Voices in the Wilderness,* translated and edited by Nikolaos S.

Hatzinikolaou. Copyright 1988 by Holy Cross
Orthodox Press.

The Lama Foundation for "For the Fires of Our
Cooking Pots."

For "Speak, Lord, For Your Servant Is Listening,"
excerpted from Creasy, William C.; pps. 55-56, from
*The Imitation of Christ: A New Reading of the 1441
Latin Autograph Manuscript.* (Mercer University Press,
1989), used by permission.

For "Acceptance," Thomas Merton: *The Asian Journal
of Thomas Merton.* Copyright © 1973 by The Merton
Legacy Trust. Reprinted by permission of New
Directions Publishing Corp.

"You Are Christ's Hands" by Saint Teresa of Avila,
reprinted from *God Makes the Rivers to Flow* by
Eknath Easwaran, © 1982, 1991 by the Blue
Mountain Center of Meditation. Courtesy of Nilgiri
Press.

Professor J. H. Kwabena Nketia, International Center
for African Music and Dance, University of Ghana,
for "Good Morning to You, God, I Am Learning."

For "Prayer of Joyful Assurance," "For the New Year,"
"May Happiness Come," "You Have Given Me All,"
"That Is the Story of Your Grace," "Prayer for Purity,"
"The Shoulders Get Tired of Carrying Sins," and
"Asking God," reprinted from *Prayer in the Religious
Tradition of Africa* by Aylward Shorter © Oxford
University Press 1975; and for "Let the Souls of Thy
People Be Cool," reprinted from *Nuer Religion* by

E. E. Evans-Pritchard © Oxford University Press 1956. Reprinted by permission of Oxford University Press.

Brother Thomas More Page, C.F.X., for "Centering Prayer." Used by permission. All rights reserved.

"Waking Up" reprinted from *Present Moment Wonderful Moment: Mindfulness Verses for Daily Living* by Thich Nhat Hanh (1990) with permission of Parallax Press, Berkeley, California.

Paulist Press for "A Prayer of Awe," "I Turn," "Love," and "For Diverse Blessings," reprinted from *The Prayers of Catherine of Siena* by Suzanne Noffke, O.P. © 1983 by Suzanne Noffke, O.P.; for "Teach Me" by Saint Anselm, reprinted from *The Fire and the Cloud* by David A. Fleming, S.M., © 1978 by The Missionary Society of St. Paul the Apostle in the state of New York; and for "Radiant Is the World Soul," reprinted from *Abraham Isaac Kook* by Ben Zion Bokser © 1978 by Ben Zion Bokser. Used by permission of Paulist Press.

The Peace Abbey and the Life Experience School for "Peace Seeds." Used by permission.

For "Tenth-Century Celtic Wish" from *A Celtic Miscellany* edited by Kenneth H. Jackson, published by Routledge and Kegan Paul Ltd. Reprinted by permission of Routledge.

Douglas Sealy for the estate of Douglas Hyde, for "The Will of God" translated by Douglas Hyde. Used by permission.

Servant Publications for "Queen of Wisdom" from *The Prayers of Saint Francis* translated by Ignatius Brady O.F.M., © 1987 by Servant Books. Published by Servant Publications, Box 8617, Ann Arbor, Michigan 48107. Used with permission.

"Sacred" by John Lame Deer reprinted with the permission of Simon & Schuster Inc. from *Lame Deer, Seeker of Visions,* by John (Fire) Lame Deer and Richard Erdoes. Copyright © 1972 by John (Fire) Lame Deer and Richard Erdoes.

Colin Smyth Limited, Publishers, and the AE Estate, for "In Quiet" from the poem "Prayer" by George W. Russell. Reprinted from *Collected Poems,* published by Colin Smyth Limited, Publishers. Used by permission.

For "His Earthly Life in Silence" by Mother Teresa of Calcutta excerpted from *In the Silence of the Heart: Reflections, Meditations, Prayers* by Mother Teresa of Calcutta, edited by Kathryn Spink, selection and arrangement copyright © Kathryn Spink 1983. Reprinted courtesy of the Society for the Promotion of Christian Knowledge (SPCK).

"Nayaz" by Hazrat Inayat Khan reprinted by permission of the Sufi Order Secretariat.

"Morning Hymn" ("Song of the Sky Loom" from *Songs of the Tewa* by Herbert Joseph Spinden) appears courtesy of Sunstone Press, Box 2321, Santa Fe, NM 87504-2321, U.S.A. Used by permission.

The Office of Tibet for the prayerful statement by His Holiness the Dalai Lama © The Office of Tibet. Reprinted by permission.

For poems by Kozan, Gitoku, Goshi and Sokin, excerpted from *Japanese Death Poems,* compiled with an introduction by Yoel Hoffmann © 1986 by Charles E. Tuttle Co., Inc. of Tokyo, Japan. Used by permission.

Barry Ulanov for "You Have Pierced My Heart" and "The Soul," from *The Prayers of Saint Augustine* by Barry Ulanov (The Seabury Press) © 1983 by Barry Ulanov. Used by permission of the author.

For prayers by John Ri, Ferreolus of Vienne, Crispina of Thagara, James Intercisus, Apollonius the Apologist, Cyprian of Carthage, Yona Kanamuzeyi, and Dietrich Bonhoeffer, taken from *Prayers of the Martyrs,* compiled and translated by Duane W. H. Arnold. Copyright © 1991 by Duane W. H. Arnold. Used by permission of Zondervan Publishing House.

Notes on Authors
and Sources

'ABDU'L-BAHÁ, 1844–1921, Bahá'í religious leader.

THE CONGREGATION OF ABRAXAS, a Unitarian Universalist order.

PHARAOH AKHENATON, d. 1358 B.C., king of Egypt who replaced old gods with sun worship.

CECIL FRANCES ALEXANDER, 1818–1895, English author.

AMERGIN, Milenesian prince who colonized Ireland many hundreds of years before Christ.

AMON RA, ancient Egyptian supreme deity.

ANSARI OF HERAT, d. 1088, Sufi poet and mystic.

SAINT ANSELM, 1033–1109, Italian-born English theologian, founder of Scholasticism.

APPOLONIUS THE APOLOGIST, d. ca. 185, early Christian martyr.

LUCIUS APULEIUS, b. ca. 125, Roman philosopher and satirist.

ARISTOTLE, 384–322 B.C., Greek philosopher, student of Plato and tutor of Alexander the Great.

GURU ARJAN, 1503–1606, fifth of the Ten Gurus of Sikhism.

SIR JACOB ASTLEY, 1579–1652, English army commander.

SAINT AUGUSTINE, BISHOP OF HIPPO, 354–430, early Christian philosopher and author, regarded as the founder of Christian theology.

JANE AUSTEN, 1775–1817, English novelist.

THE AVESTA OR ZENDAVESTA, the sacred text of Zoroastrianism.

BABYLONIAN TALMUD, OR TALMUD BABLI, ca. sixth century B.C., an authoritative version of the Jewish law. (Another is the Talmud Yerushalmi, or Jerusalem Talmud). See "Talmud" below.

BAHÁ'U'LLÁH, 1817–1892, Persian religious leader (born Mirza Husayn Ali Nur), founder of Bahá'ísm.

BLESSED MARIAM BAOUARDY, 1846–1878, Galilean-born Carmelite mystic, called The Little Arab.

LYNN BAQUIE, American member of Fellowship in Prayer.

KARL BARTH, 1886–1968, Swiss protestant theologian.

SAINT BASIL (THE GREAT), 330?–378?, Greek Christian leader, Bishop of Caesarea.

KATHERINE LEE BATES, 1859–1929, author of "America."

LUDWIG VAN BEETHOVEN, 1770–1827, German composer.

SAINT BENEDICT, d. ca. 547, founder of Christian monasticism.

DIETRICH BONHOEFFER, 1906–1945, Lutheran pastor, hanged by the Nazis.

THE BOOK OF SONGS, ancient Chinese compilation of poems.

THE BOOK OF COMMON PRAYER, compilation of prayers and liturgy used in the Anglican Church.

WALTER RUSSELL BOWIE, 1882–1969, American Episcopal priest.

SIR THOMAS BROWNE, 1605–1682, English physician and Christian author.

ELIZABETH BARRETT BROWNING, 1806–1861, English poet.

ROBERT BURNS, 1759–1796, Scottish national poet.

CAEDMON, fl. 670, lay brother at an English monastery, early English poet.

AMY CARMICHAEL, 1868–1951, missionary to Japan and India.

THE CARMINA GADELICA, a collection of ancient Celtic spiritual verse.

SAINT CATHERINE OF SIENA, 1347–1380, Italian religious leader and political mediator.

THE CHANDOGYA UPANISHAD, Hindu philosophical commentary on the Vedas.

RICHARD OF CHICHESTER, 1197–1253, Richard de Wych, Bishop of Chichester.

CHINOOK PSALTER, twentieth century, wisdom of the native peoples of the American Pacific Northwest.

SAINT CLEMENT OF ROME, d. ca. 95, one of the early Christian Fathers, Pope (89–97) and martyr.

THE CLOUD OF UNKNOWING, fourteenth century, English mystical treatise.

HENRY SLOANE COFFIN, 1877–1954, American Presbyterian pastor.

THE OFFICE FOR COMPLINE, Christian evening prayer before retiring.

CRISPINA OF THAGARA, d. 304, early Christian martyr.

CYPRIAN OF CARTHAGE, d. 258, early Christian martyr.

SAINT CYRIL, fifth century, saint of the Coptic Church.

THE DALAI LAMA, 1935– , leader of Tibetan Buddhism, winner of the Nobel Peace Prize.

DANTE ALIGHIERI, 1265–1321, Italian renaissance poet, author of *The Divine Comedy*.

LAMA SURYA DAS, 1950– , American Dzogchen lama.

DEVADAS, late seventeenth century, Hindu poet and saint.

SAINT DIMITRI OF ROSTOV, seventeenth century, Russian saint.

DINKAR, ca. 1628–ca. 1695, Hindu poet and saint.

DNYANADEV, fl. 1290, Hindu poet and saint.

JOHN DONNE, 1572–1631, English poet, ordained late in life.

SIR FRANCIS DRAKE, 1540–1596, English explorer and naval hero.

MEISTER ECKHART, ca. 1260–ca.1328, German Dominican mystic and theologian

EKNATH, 1548–1600, Hindu poet and saint.

BLESSED ELIZABETH OF THE TRINITY, 1880–1906, French nun.

SAINT EPHRAIM THE SYRIAN, 303–373, early theologian of the Eastern Church.

DESIDERIUS ERASMUS, 1467–1536, Dutch humanist, Roman Catholic priest, and important figure of the Renaissance.

EURIPIDES, 480?–406 B.C., classical Greek dramatist.

THE FATIHAH ("THE OPENING"), a daily Muslim prayer, from the Qur'an.

FRANÇOIS DE SALIGNAC DE LA MOTHE-FÉNELON, 1651–1715, French clergyman and writer.

FERREOLUS OF VIENNE, third century, Christian martyr.

ARTHUR STANLEY THEODORE FISHER, English scholar and poet.

GEORGE FOX, 1624–1691, founder of the Society of Friends (the Quakers).

SAINT FRANCIS OF ASSISI, 1182?–1226, Italian Roman Catholic monk, founder of the Franciscan order.

GALLICAN SACRAMENTARY, historical rite within the Catholic Church.

GELASIAN SACRAMENTARY, order of service

associated with Pope Gelasius (elected 492); earliest written versions date to the eighth century.

CHIEF DAN GEORGE, of the Tell-lall-wwatt Indians (Canada). Oscar nominee for *Little Big Man*, environmental spokesman.

BHAGAVAD GITA, Hindu sacred poem in which Krishna instructs the prince Arjuna in spiritual wisdom.

GITOKU, 1701–1754, Japanese haiku poet.

GOSHI, 1739–1775, Japanese haiku poet.

DOM AELRED GRAHAM, 1905– , American Catholic writer.

GREGORIAN SACRAMENTARY, eighth century, liturgy named after Pope Gregory I (ca. 540–604).

JUDAH HALEVI, ca. 1075–1141, Jewish poet and philosopher.

JOSEPH HALL, 1574–1656, Bishop of Norwich, England.

THICH NHAT HANH, Vietnamese Buddhist monk.

JACQUETTA HOPKINS HAWKES, 1910– , English author.

GEORGE HERBERT, 1593–1633, Anglican priest and poet whose religious verse forms the basis of several Christian hymns.

RABBI ABRAHAM HESCHEL, 1907–1972, Polish-born Hasidic rabbi and writer.

HEZEKIAH, r. ca. 707 B.C., king of Judah.

SAINT HILDEGARD OF BINGEN, 1098–1179, German Christian mystic.

WINIFRED HOLTBY, 1898–1935, English novelist.

GERARD MANLEY HOPKINS, 1844–1889, English poet and Jesuit priest.

CHARLES HOWE, 1661–1745, English writer.

SAINT IGNATIUS OF LOYOLA, 1491–1556, founder of the Jesuits.

JAMES INTERCISUS, d. ca. 420, early Christian martyred in Persia.

ISAIAH, eighth century B.C., major Hebrew prophet, nobleman of the kingdom of Judah.

FRANCIS JAMMES, 1868–1938, French poet.

JESUS OF NAZARETH, 4? B.C.– 30? A.D., Jewish teacher and prophet believed by Christians to be the Son of God.

JEWISH TEMPLE BLESSING, seventh century B.C., in the book of Numbers, chapter 6, verses 24–26.

SAINT JOHN "THE EVANGELIST" (OR "THE DIVINE"), first century, one of the Twelve Apostles of

Jesus, traditionally considered the author of the fourth Gospel.

SAMUEL JOHNSON, 1709–1784, English writer and lexicographer.

JULIAN OF NORWICH, 1342–1420, mystic, considered by some to be England's first woman of letters.

HAZRAT INAYAT KHAN, 1882–1927, founder of the Sufi order in the West.

YONA KANAMUZEYI, 1918–1964, Anglican priest shot in Rwanda.

BUNJIRO KAWATE, 1814–1883, Japanese Shintoist, founder of the Konko-Kyo sect.

BISHOP THOMAS KEN, 1637–1711, Bishop of Bath and Wells.

JOHN KETTLEWELL, 1653–1695, English Christian writer.

SØREN KIERKEGAARD, 1813–1855, Danish religious writer and philosopher.

MARTIN LUTHER KING, JR., 1929–1968, African-American civil rights crusader, pastor and martyr; winner of the Nobel Peace Prize.

JOHN KNOX, 1513–1572, Scottish reformer.
KOZAN, eighteenth century, Zen poet.

JOHN LAME DEER, Sioux Indian.

LEOFRIC, BISHOP OF EXETER, eleventh century, English liturgist.

LEONINE SACRAMENTARY, fifth century, an early rite within the Catholic Church, named after Pope Leo the Great (p. 440–461).

ABRAHAM LINCOLN, 1809–1865, sixteenth president of the United States.

SAINT LUKE, first century, physician and author of the third Gospel.

MARTIN LUTHER, 1483–1546, German theologian and leader of the Protestant Reformation.

MAHĪPATI, b. 1715, Hindu poet.

MAIMONIDES, 1135–1204, Jewish rabbi, scholar and physician.

MANCHÁN OF LIATH, a medieval Irish wirter.

RAISSA MARITAIN, 1883–1960, French Jewish mystic, convert to Catholicism.

SAINT MARK, first century, one of the Twelve Apostles of Jesus, traditionally considered the author of the second Gospel.

THE MARRANOS OR "NEW CHRISTIANS," Jewish converts to Christianity and their descendants in

Spain and Portugal, harshly persecuted in the fourteenth and fifteenth centuries.

PETER MARSHALL, 1902–1949, chaplain to the United States Congress.

SAINT MATTHEW, first century, one of the Twelve Apostles of Jesus, traditionally accepted author of the first Gospel.

MAYŪRA, early seventh century, Sanskrit poet.

THOMAS MERTON, 1915–1968, French-born American Trappist monk (later priest) and writer.

F. B. MEYER, 1847–1929, American Baptist preacher and educator.

JOHN MILTON, 1608–1674, English poet.

THOMAS MORE, 1478–1535, English statesman and Roman Catholic martyr executed by Henry VIII.

THE MOZARABIC LITURGY AND MOZARABIC BOOK OF ORDERS, before 700 A.D., one of the rites in the Roman Catholic Church in the West.

MUHAMMAD, ca. 570–632, prophet and founder of Islam.

RABBI NACHMAN OF BRATZLAV, 1772–1811, Polish-born Hasidic teacher and storyteller.

JOHN MASON NEALE, 1818–1866, Anglican clergyman.

ADMIRAL LORD NELSON, 1758–1805, English fleet commander.

JOHN HENRY NEWMAN, 1801–1890, English cardinal and theologian, a founder of the Oxford Movement.

REINHOLD NIEBUHR, 1892–1971, American theologian and political activist.

NOAH THE MUSLIM, Islamic sage.

HENRI NOUWEN, Dutch-born priest and author.

A NUN'S PRAYER, seventeenth century, author unknown.

BROTHER THOMAS MORE PAGE, C.F.X., b. 1916, American member of the Brothers of Saint Francis Xavier.

BLAISE PASCAL, 1623–1662, French mathematician.

SAINT PATRICK, 390?–461?, patron saint of Ireland.

JEAN PAUL, 1763–1825, German novelist.

JOHN PAUL II, 1920–, Pope of the Roman Catholic Church (1978–)

SAINT PAUL OF TARSUS, 5?–64? or 67?, a Jew and Roman citizen who became a Christian apostle to the Gentiles.

PADRAIC PEARSE, 1879–1916, Irish poet, essayist

and playwright, executed for his leading role in the Easter Rising.

WILLIAM PENN, 1644–1718, English Quaker who founded the colony of Pennsylvania in America.

PLATO, 427?–347 B.C., Greek philosopher, student of Socrates.

PLINY THE ELDER, ca. 23–79, Roman writer and naturalist.

PRIMER OF 1559, in the book Private Prayers of the Reign of Queen Elizabeth, published by the Parker Society, 1851.

PSALMS, OR PSALTER, compiled ca. 550–ca. 100 B.C., an Old Testament book of 150 sacred songs.

THE QUR'AN, the sacred text of Islam, containing God's revelations to Muhammad, divided into 114 sūras (chapters).

RÁBI'A, ca. 717–801, Islamic woman mystic.

SRI RAMAKRISHNA, 1836–1886, Hindu mystic.

RAMDAS, 1608–1681, Hindu poet and saint.

WALTER RAUSCHENBUSCH, 1861–1918, American pastor and leader of the Social Gospel movement.

JOHN RI, d. 1839, Roman Catholic missionary martyred in Korea.

CHRISTINA ROSSETTI, 1830–1894, English poet and lyricist, emphasizing religious themes.

JALALU'D-DIN RÚMÍ, Sufi poet.

GEORGE RUSSELL, 1867–1935, Irish nationalist who wrote under the pen name "AE."

SHEIKH SAADI, 1184–1291, Sufi poet.

SAMUEL, eleventh century B.C., Hebrew judge and prophet.

SANAI, d. ca. 1150, Sana'i al-Ghaznavi, Persian poet.

SAINT SARRAH, late fourth century, Libyan ascetic and saint.

THE SARUM BREVIARY, Latin missal from the English medieval cathedral town of Sarum (Salisbury).

ALBERT SCHWEITZER, 1875–1965, French physician, missionary and writer, winner of the Nobel Peace Prize.

SAINT SERAPHIM, 1759–1883, Russian Orthodox mystic and leader.

WILLIAM SHAKESPEARE, 1564–1616, English playwright and poet.

THE BODHICARYAVATARA OF SHANTIDEVA, eighth century, Buddhist scripture.

GEORGE BERNARD SHAW, 1856–1950, Irish-born British playwright.

THE SHEMA, Deuteronomy 6:4 et. seq., ancient Jewish affirmation of faith.

SAMUEL FRANCIS SMITH, 1808–1895, American poet.

SOKIN, d. 1818, Japanese haiku poet.

CHARLES H. SPURGEON, 1834–1892, English Baptist clergyman.

ROBERT LOUIS STEVENSON, 1850–1894, Scottish novelist, poet and essayist.

THE LOTUS SUTRA, ancient Buddhist text.

RABINDRANATH TAGORE, 1861–1941, Bengali poet and writer on Hindu spirituality.

THE TALMUD, the fundamental compilation of Jewish oral law.

THE TAO-TE-CHING, third century B.C. (?), Chinese philosophical book.

"TAPS," nineteenth century, words to the U.S. military bugle call for sunset by an unknown author.

JEREMY TAYLOR, 1613–1667, English theologian, bishop of Down and Connor in Ireland.

ALFRED, LORD TENNYSON, 1809–1892, English poet. The prayer in this volume is from his *Morte D'Arthur*.

SAINT TERESA OF AVILA, 1515–1582, Spanish nun and mystic, founder of the Carmelite order.

MOTHER TERESA OF CALCUTTA, 1910– , Albanian-born Indian nun, founder of the Missionaries of Charity, winner of the Nobel Peace Prize.

TEWA PUEBLO INDIANS, native peoples of northern New Mexico.

THEOPHAN "THE RECLUSE," 1815–1894, Catholic monk and mystic.

SAINT THÉRÈSE OF LISIEUX, 1873–1897, French nun known as "the Little Flower."

SAINT THOMAS AQUINAS, 1226–1274, Italian theologian, prominent figure of Scholasticism.

THOMAS À KEMPIS, 1380–1471, German monk, Augustinian priest in the Netherlands.

PAUL TILLICH, 1886–1965, German-born American theologian and philosopher.

THE TORAH, (in Hebrew, "law" or "teaching"), the Pentateuch, the first five books of the Bible.

TUKĀRĀM, 1608–1649, Hindu poet.

THE VEDAS, compiled ca. 1000–ca. 500 B.C., the

oldest Hindu sanskrit texts, consisting of the Samhita, the Brahmanas, the Aranyakas, and the Upanishads.

THE ATHARVA VEDA, a compilation of magic spells, contained in the Samhita (see "The Vedas" above).

THE RIG VEDA, ancient Hindu sacred verses, contained in the Samhita (see "The Vedas" above).

ISAAC WATTS, 1674–1748, English theologian, poet and hymnist.

CHARLES WESLEY, 1707–1788, prolific English hymnist, brother of John Wesley.

JOHN WESLEY, 1703–1791, English preacher, founder of Methodism.

WILLIAM WHITING, 1825–1878, hymnist.

JOHN GREENLEAF WHITTIER, 1807–1892, American poet.

WILLIAM WORDSWORTH, 1770–1850, English poet.

LEVI YITZCHAK OF BERDITCHEV, 1740–1809, Hasidic leader.

ZOROASTER, OR ZARATHUSTRA, ca. 628–ca. 551 B.C., Persian prophet and teacher, founder of Zoroastrianism.

Subject Index

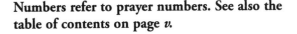

Numbers refer to prayer numbers. See also the table of contents on page _v_.

About Fellowship in Prayer

Fellowship in Prayer, the interfaith journal, has an international readership in over 80 countries. Each issue offers the spiritual insights, practices, and beliefs of women and men from a broad spectrum of the world's faith traditions.

The emphasis is on the individual writer's personal experience of the sacred dimension as she or he has experienced it in his or her own life. The authors range from the very well known, such as Matthew Fox, Thich Nhat Hanh, Brother David Steindl-Rast, and the Dalai Lama, to "ordinary" people who have had transforming experiences that changed their lives.

If you would like a free copy of *Fellowship in Prayer,* write to:

Fellowship in Prayer
291 Witherspoon Street
Princeton, NJ 08542-3227
U.S.A.